What is the potential for educational collaboration in the single European market? Education in and about the media is expanding across Europe and, like the industries it studies, is changing rapidly. The future of media education is a matter of live concern in all European countries, as educators and practitioners throughout the continent come together to learn from each other and to plan for the changes to come.

Media Education Across Europe identifies the exciting developments now taking place within and across European boundaries. Essays from eight different nations – the UK, France, Germany, Italy, Spain, Belgium, Sweden and the Netherlands – explore the development of courses and approaches to the subject in each country. The contributors also consider the prospects for European collaboration in media education; the possibilities opening up for graduate employment; and the future conflict – and co-operation – between media teachers and media employers.

The editors: **David French** is Director of the Communications Studies Centre at Coventry University and Chair of the European Communication Group. **Michael Richards** is Vice Principal and Professor at Worcester College of Higher Education and Joint Chair of the Standing Conference of Cultural, Communication and Media Studies.

The contributors: David French, Michael Richards, Pier Paolo Giglioli, Macu Alvarez, Frieda Saeys, Yves Winkin, Jan Ove Eriksson, Ard Heuvelman, Axel Gryspeerdt, Klaus Merten, Jeanne-Marie Barberis.

Media education across Europe

Edited by David French
and
Michael Richards

Published in association with the
Broadcasting Standards Council
5–8 The Sanctuary
London SW1P 3JS
Telephone: 071 233 0544
FAX: 071 233 0397

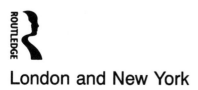

London and New York

First published 1994
by Routledge
11 New Fetter Lane, London EC4P 4EE

Simultaneously published in the USA and Canada
by Routledge
29 West 35th Street, New York, NY 10001

Phototypeset in Times by Intype, London

Printed and bound in Great Britain by T.J. Press (Padstow) Ltd, Padstow,
Cornwall
Printed on acid free paper

British Library Cataloguing in Publication Data
A catalogue record for this book is available from the British Library.

Library of Congress Cataloging in Publication Data
Media education across Europe / edited by David French and Michael
Richards
   p. cm.
'Published in association with the Broadcasting Standards Council.'
Includes bibliographical references (p.) and index.
1. Communication–Study and teaching–Europe. 2. Mass media–Study
and teaching—Europe. I. French, David, 1946–. II. Richards, Michael,
1945–.
P91.5.E85M43 1993
302.2.'0704–dc20   93–1600
                                                                CIP

ISBN 0-415-10016-X (hbk)
ISBN 0-415-10017-8 (pbk)

To Ralph Pearce and others who share with him the credit for initiating media education in European universities

Contents

Part III

Tables

Contributors

Macu Alvarez combines academic work at the University of the Basque Country with a continuing career in journalism. She is currently completing research at the City University, London.

Jeanne-Marie Barberis is a leading figure in the research group Praxiling at the University of Montpellier III. Her particular interests are in the analysis of televisual texts.

Jan Ove Eriksson is Head of the Department of Sociology at the University of Karlstad and has been director of the study programme in communication, with a particular interest in communication in organisations.

David French is Director of the Centre for Communication Studies at Coventry University. He has lengthy experience of teaching in media policy and particular interest in European collaboration for curriculum development and student exchanges.

Pier Paolo Giglioli is Professor of Sociology at the Istituto di Discipline della Comunicazione at the University of Bologna, the leading Italian department for teaching and research in the subject. He is now particularly concerned with the sociology of culture, media and political legitimacy.

Axel Gryspeerdt is Professor of Communication, specialising in public relations and organisational communication, at the Catholic University of Louvain (French-speaking). His special concerns are with social and symbolic representations, with contemporary belief systems and the circulation and mediation of ideas.

Ard Heuvelman teaches psychology and mass communication at the University of Twente and is project leader with the audience research department of the Netherlands Broadcasting Corporation. He is particularly interested in the cognitive and affective effects of television.

Klaus Merten is Professor of Empirical Communication Research at the University of Münster and has published widely in communication theory, methodology and applied communication research. He has visiting posts at numerous German universities.

Michael Richards is Professor and Vice-Principal at Worcester College of Higher Education and was previously course leader of one of the leading British courses in communication. He chaired the Communication and Cultural Studies Board of CNAA and is Joint Chair of the Standing Conference of Cultural, Communication and Media Studies.

Frieda Saeys is Professor of Communication Science at the University of Ghent, with particular teaching interests in media history, methodology, broadcasting systems and audiovisual practice. Her research interests are in the mass media and privacy and the reception of televisual information.

Yves Winkin is currently Professor at the University of Liège and the University of Louvain. He has broad teaching interests and experience in course development, specialising in the relationship between anthropology and communication. He has active associations with the CNRS (Paris) and numerous universities across the world.

Preface

This book has its origins in a colloquium at the University of the Basque Country in May 1992. The chapters which reflect on national experiences are developed from papers given at that meeting and the rest of the book owes a great deal to discussions which took place there. The book does not set out to provide a comprehensive description of media education even in the countries represented. Any attempt to do so would become rapidly out of date. Rather, it displays arguments which are important in the countries concerned. Needless to say all chapters represent the views of individual authors, not the official positions of their universities.

Grateful thanks are due to all those who helped with the meeting, including the Broadcasting Standards Council, which provided much of the funding, and the Universities of the Basque Country and of Karlstad. Particular thanks go to those representatives of the media professions from whose advice the discussion at the colloquium gained great benefit: Roger Bolton and Eduard Boet from broadcast journalism, and Colin Shaw and Andrea Millwood Hargrave of the Broadcasting Standards Council.

Part I

Chapter 1

Introduction

David French and Michael Richards

This book has two main objectives. It seeks to compare the practice of university media and communication education in a number
of European countries and to explore and develop the potential
for collaboration in the subject across the continent at higher
education level. Alongside these main concerns it also offers some
reflection about the development of the subject area as an increasingly coherent field.

The objectives are interwoven throughout the book. While the
main purpose of the national chapters is comparative, they also
address the objective of European collaboration. Illustrating as
they do the range of issues and materials with which partners in
any joint venture will have to come to terms, these chapters necessarily vary in style. Some emphasise the role of national trends
and policies, some that of individual institutions, and some display
arguments and examples which inform individual courses.

Both objectives are difficult and the book can only partially
achieve them. To produce a full comparison would require each
national account to be an identically structured and comprehensive picture. Such accounts would be hard to compile and would
be likely to miss the individual qualities of particular countries.
They would also be snapshots, concealing the turbulence of the
subject. Communication is a field in constant flux and the choice
here has been to opt for individual accounts which directly address
processes of change and development.

Similarly, to achieve real European collaboration is not easy.
Too often questions about practice 'abroad' are dealt with in ways
whose crudity would not be tolerated in analyses of one's 'own'
country. If courses are to develop common curricula, in whole or
in part, then the accumulation of a stock of material about the

operation of communication processes in other countries is a requirement needing urgent attention. Such initiatives are otherwise likely to remain simply empty tokens of ill-considered intent.

The same is true of measures such as student exchange schemes. If students are to take full advantage of opportunities to study abroad, and the ERASMUS programme of European student mobility has given many the chance to do so, then they and the academics who organise their programmes need a familiarity with educational practice in partner countries and institutions.

These objectives were formulated at a meeting of academics and practitioners which took place at the University of the Basque County, Bilbao, in May 1992. Many of those involved in the meeting had shared the experience of building and operating a successful ERASMUS programme of student exchange in communication studies. The Bilbao meeting was motivated by the view that it was time to take stock, to share experience and to consider the direction of the subject's development. A main conclusion of the meeting was that those presently involved in it have to take a main share of the responsibility for this development and the present book is a contribution to that.

The national chapters grow out of papers presented at the Bilbao meeting and the remainder of the book is based on themes which arose in discussion. It was very clear that, not only was there a considerable commonality of approach and intellectual orientation among those present but that participants shared the view that the subject is passing through a distinctive and exciting phase. It is becoming an increasingly important part of higher education while at the same time achieving greater social and academic coherence.

Another major theme to emerge was the importance of teaching as a semi-autonomous force in the development of the subject, alongside and drawing upon research, but opening up new issues and applications for core theories and analyses.

Observations such as these provided a backdrop against which the specific objectives of the meeting were pursued. The same balance is present in this book.

It would be hard to invent a topic more likely to excite scepticism among academic traditionalists than European collaboration in the study of communication and the media. The historic distrust of popular taste which still characterises much establishment response to the media themselves has transferred to a too easy dismissal, as passing fashion, of the heavy student demand for education about communication. It is important to persuade those who take this view, whether within or outside the university, that behind these market pressures lies an important intellectual opportunity. But the difficulty of doing this is increased by the fact that students seeking entry to communication and media courses may be turning their backs upon courses offered by others who often have powerful positions in the university system.

European collaboration, although also a growth point in all universities, is also still often regarded sceptically. This chapter is being written in June 1993, shortly after the passage of the Maastricht Treaty through the House of Commons and the Danish referendum on the Treaty. But the European Monetary System remains in a state of uncertainty, symbolising the popular ambivalence towards European institutions.

The mission of the book is, above all, to confront such scepticism. The study of the media and communication has arrived and is increasingly well entrenched in the curricula of European universities. Its future will be strengthened by increased collaboration between universities across national frontiers, with as open as possible a trade in students, course materials and ideas. As the institutions of the 'invisible college' – academic associations, journals, study groups and so on – grow it is important that they do so in an open way across Europe. The next chapter begins to unravel some of the complexities of this task.

Chapter 2

The European agenda
Rhetoric and reality

David French and Michael Richards

In most Western European countries, those twin repositories of cultural capital, the universities and the national communication media, are experiencing major change. Some parallels are very striking: both frequently find themselves facing the perils and opportunities of the market for the first time. But, detailed similarities and differences aside, it is very important that both now find themselves having to re-examine their basic assumptions.

One key theme of this book is that, in their common crisis, the media and the universities have often begun to look at each other in rather different ways. As is described in Chapter 14, whereas formerly interaction has often been made rather difficult, the climate has begun to look more favourable. This is not uniform across the continent; as some of the national chapters make clear, the attitudes of academics and practitioners are quite complex and changes of position are in each case mediated by a whole set of institutional political processes. But there is a real sense in which those involved in education about the media and communication, wherever they are in Europe, now find themselves confronting many of the same issues as they plan and deliver their courses. Not only do they share a more or less common intellectual tradition, they also have to deal with many of the same problems in their own institutions and in those they study.

One of those common properties is, of course, that which is labelled 'Europe', with all its complex ambiguities. To evaluate some of the significance of 'Europe' in the present and future of communication education is the purpose of this chapter.

Between the planning of the meeting in Spain which inspired this book and the writing of the manuscript, economic and political events have dramatically demonstrated the absurdity of any simplistic notions about the meaning of European integration and the process which may be leading towards it. The currency crises of the autumn of 1992 and their consequences for political relationships within, between and beyond the member states of the European Community have highlighted the differences in view over the long-term identity of Europe. The referenda in Denmark and France and evidence about public uncertainty elsewhere display the differences between rulers and the ruled in many countries. These concerns have not died with the departure from power of Margaret Thatcher, as might at one time have seemed to be the case.

Fortunately for us the need is not to engage in a detailed analysis of the 'macro' issues in this debate. The second major concern of this book is indeed with 'Europe' as it impinges upon education about communication and the media, but this concern, in effect, reduces to two relatively prosaic questions.

The first concerns the present: in courses of higher education around Europe, what are the real similarities and differences in content and philosophy? In other words, are such courses drawing together in a way which is favourable to co-operation between them? This question is addressed chiefly in the national chapters, with some implications being picked up in the synthesising discussions in the last part of the book.

The remainder of this chapter introduces the second question which then will recur throughout the remaining chapters: in what ways is the subject in the future likely to incorporate European issues and experiences within the curriculum which it offers its students?

After all, in many respects the concept of Europe should loom large in all areas of the tertiary curriculum. The year 1992 saw a key phase in the race to prepare students for careers in the European Community, leading to a much greater freedom of movement throughout the Community, including entry to higher education and employment. Major steps have been taken towards the mutual recognition of qualifications. Education Ministers spent some time during 1992 discussing the important part which higher education could play in cementing relations with European neighbours, those discussions centring on the need for greater student mobility and improved language competence and extensions to community programmes like ERASMUS and LINGUA. The agenda also included consideration of ways of improving access to higher education, for both school-leavers and more mature students, with common targets for participation in higher education in the Community. At present participation rates vary widely, with France and Germany at the top and Britain towards the bottom of the league table of those taking part in education and training after the age of 16. There were also discussions centring on the need for closer links between higher education and industry, and the potential for extending community programmes like COMETT, designed to bridge the higher education/industry divide.

Of all university subjects, the study of communication and the media should perhaps take the lead in addressing European issues. It is a new field and its rapid growth has coincided with the period in which 'Europe' has come to dominate the political, economic, social and cultural agendas. It seems natural to expect that the subject should take to its heart a development of such importance.

A particularly powerful inducement to do so might seem to come from the increasingly European orientation of the industries and professional practices which the subject addresses.

THE COMMUNICATION INDUSTRIES

The increasing concern with 'Europe' has been a major feature of debates and action within media policy through the 1980s and on into the 1990s. But closer scrutiny reveals a significant gap between the rhetoric and the reality.

It is an area in which the European Community has been particularly active. Not only are the media seen as a sector of economic importance in competition with the United States and Japan, but they are also taken to be crucial in developing the 'citizen's Europe'. They are seen as a means to encourage the people of Europe to develop some elements of a common identity, thinking European as well as being more likely to enter the European market-place as consumers and workers from wherever in Europe they may come.

So the Community has promoted the MEDIA programme, giving financial support to, for example, projects in co-production, sub-titling and dubbing (see, e.g., Langham Brown and Luyken, 1990). Similarly the Community, with a whole range of other multinational European institutions, has been active in promoting pan-European regulatory regimes to ensure that cross-frontier broadcasting can take place without encountering obstacles from national sensitivities (see Blumler 1992: Chapters 2 and 12).

Alongside these evidences of pro-active initiatives at the level of official European institutions have been the activities of commercial entrepreneurs. The cable television viewer throughout Europe can, should she or he choose, watch many of the same channels with little or no interference by national regulators.

The situation is similar in the closely allied industries such as public relations and advertising, which are important here not least because they employ a large proportion of graduates in the subject. The major companies all have offices throughout Europe, often co-ordinated by a headquarters in Brussels, and pan-European campaigns have been a major talking point in the conferences and trade journals.

The gap between such heady aspirations and reality is well documented. The new cable channels are often very clearly oriented towards particular national markets; television consumers show clear preferences for domestically originated programming and pan-European advertising campaigns remain of marginal importance.

But the significance of this credibility gap should not be overestimated. 'Europe', whatever it may specifically signify, has entered the consciousness of those with influence over and within the media and communication industries. Furthermore, if the reality of new pan-European communication activity falls somewhat short of expectations, its anticipated importance has been a serious contributory factor in destabilising the old institutional structures. To give a British example, the new regime for commercial television, introduced in 1993, and the changes envisaged with the new BBC charter due in 1996, are all largely predicated on the imminence of an invasion of cross-frontier broadcasting which would fatally damage any broadcasting system conceived purely in national terms.[1] The realities that BSkyB, the satellite service, has presented a product constructed almost entirely in terms of the British national market and that most other European countries have had a long experience of dealing with cross-frontier broadcasting are post facto irrelevancies. The key issues are that within these industries 'Europe' has come to be perceived as a major issue and that this perception is an important dimension of the way in which they will continue to impinge upon university courses.

EUROPE IN THE COMMUNICATION CURRICULUM

There is no systematic evidence about the extent to which 'Europe' has penetrated the content of university courses. To draw confident conclusions would require not only a detailed analysis of syllabuses but also a study of how these syllabuses are drawn upon in delivery. Nevertheless, the question remains an important one and one with which those concerned with the direction of course development in the subject should take seriously. In these circumstances the finding of one small-scale piece of research may be useful, even though it is confined to Britain and deals with secondary schools rather than universities.

At the time of writing, there are four GCE 'A' level syllabuses available in Media Studies in Britain, and many schools and colleges have taken them up. GCSE programmes have also been introduced, and elements of media education are to be found in the National Curriculum. Media Studies syllabuses seem to contain opportunities for developing an explicit European focus through their overall aims. For example, at 'A' level many syllabuses encourage candidates to be aware of media systems in different cultures, through, for example, studies of the media and cultural imperialism, new media technologies, regulation and de-regulation, and public service broadcasting. But these opportunities are rarely taken up in syllabus exemplars or notes of guidance issued to teachers. Where there are specific references to national contexts, these tend to be related to Britain, for example to British broadcasting, or to the British Independent Film and Video Movement, and of course occasionally to the USA, the outstanding example being the Hollywood Studio system. This is a problem not of ethnocentricity, but rather of blindness to specifically European examples as compared with those from other countries and perhaps of the generally low priority attached to the whole range of international topics.

As an illustration, in one syllabus a series of specimen examination questions is offered to teachers. One is tantalisingly international: it reads 'Explain how one of the following challenges the appeal of North American film and television: TV Globo, ICAIC, the Indian film industry in Bombay, Egyptian cinema and television production' (UCLES 1990:21). This specimen question offers an extraordinary range of examples with which students can work, yet none is specifically concerned with policy and practice in mainland Europe.

The same Examining Board offers another version of its GCE
'A' level Media Studies syllabus. In its section on media institutions, the syllabus refers to

> concepts of the alternative and independent as revealed in case
> studies of (a) the alternative press or working-class publishing,
> British Independent Film and Video workshop movement; and
> (b) a non-UK media industry, such as Asian popular cinema,
> or Jamaican music industry, or southern African broadcast sys-
> tems, or Eastern Bloc news production.
>
> (UCLES 1990: 21)

Furthermore, in the media debate section of the syllabus, candidates are encouraged to present case studies of the practices and
debates associated with two of the following: American
expressionism, film-noir, British documentary movement, European avant-garde practices, melodrama, British video practices
with special attention to black film and video-making, television
drama, teenage magazines, children's comics and television, drama
or documentary. The effect therefore, is to permit the study of
European dimensions but only rarely to give it active encourage-
ment, and, given the pressure on the teaching timetable, this can
be expected effectively to exclude their substantial discussion.

The low profile given to European issues looks likely to continue
in the future. One syllabus (UCLES 1991:3) still refers in its
media institutions sections to the 'media sociology of British media
institutions', although there is reference to the 'international
organisation of the press and image markets', but no specific
steerage to European dimensions within this. Chasing through the
media institutions sections of the syllabus, we find other opportunities to encourage European dimensions which remain unfulfilled.
For example, candidates are encouraged to undertake case studies
in two of four areas; three of these relate to Britain, the other to
the USA. Case studies are also a feature of the media debates
section of the syllabus, where candidates are required to undertake
them in relation to two of nine areas. Only one of these is specifically European, and concerns only European avant-garde practices. Furthermore, a generally comprehensive list of resources
attached to the syllabus for teachers neglects important sources
of work with a European focus, most noticeably the *European
Journal of Communication*.

There is no conceptual reason why media studies should, as it has developed in Britain, not be readily able to address European subjects. That it does not do so to any great extent is a function of the lack of priority and of intellectual resources devoted to such topics. To deal with such issues requires a change of focus. The analysis of European communication in part involves the making of comparisons, to reveal similarities, differences and continuities, but nothing about this is new; within countries comparisons are continually made between different types of media, or between historical periods. If there is something distinctive about addressing the European level, it is in the need to consider the ways in which national media structures belong to an international media system. The exploration of the nature of this system ought to be a pre-requisite of any internationally oriented work – indeed, it is impossible to make full sense of any national media system without placing it in the international context.

The extent to which British media studies in both curriculum content and until recently in research has neglected the properties of the international system is an indicator of how far it remains trapped in ethnocentric, nationalistic blinkers; in the countries of the European mainland it is less easy to ignore the realities of, for example, cross-frontier broadcasting. Yet – and this we must emphasise – to analyse the nature of the system does not require new theories or concepts; all that is required is the dedication of intellectual resources to this neglected subject matter. Even simple comparisons offer potential. Not only would a comparison of, for example, the production context of the BBC, RTBF and RAI be informative about the range of European possibilities, it would also serve the important function of revealing taken-for-granted assumptions about the British system. Such comparative work is beginning to be an important feature of academic media studies, but its development has come only recently in the growth of the subject and the unrealised potential remains considerable. Moreover, the fact that comparative European issues are now being taken up in academic research is no guarantee that they will be widely reflected in the curriculum; indeed, the patchy and late development of such issues as research topics undermines the likelihood of their widespread take-up. There is perhaps an irony in the fact that European intellectual thought and ideas are present in British communication and media syllabuses and have in fact been influenced by experience of communication and media practices in Europe. It remains true, however, that there is little direct emphasis on the very systems and organisations which provided a framework for the development of those ideas.

This is a study of practice in British schools. However, its implications have a wider importance. One reason is because the school curriculum in Britain is often designed by, and almost always reflects the attitudes of, university academics. If a neglect of the international dimension is found in schools then it is also likely to occur in British university courses.

However, curriculum design is determined by factors which are probably of still greater significance. First, successful courses depend upon access to adequate supporting literature for staff and students. The preponderant availability of American texts and research reports probably makes it inevitable that, where access to the English language is not a problem, courses will lean heavily upon such material whether or not the inclinations of course designers might point elsewhere.

Second, as theories of communication increasingly recognise the process of communication as a circuit, in which the production of a text, the text itself and its consumption are inextricably linked, the issues involved in successful international comparisons become far more complex. While there is still a tendency to analyse texts in themselves (partly explaining the greater propensity of, for example, courses in film and cinema to address material of international origin), if production or consumption is to be taken seriously, the cultural judgements required are extremely demanding.

If it can be assumed that these factors occur more widely, then it follows that whatever protestations about the importance of 'Europe' may be uttered by educational policy-makers, the reality will fall short. There is, we suggest, a common need to develop the materials and methods which will support comparative studies and this can probably only be achieved by the collaborative efforts of academics from different European countries.

STUDENT EXCHANGES AND THE EXPERIENCE OF 'EUROPE'

Curriculum development as discussed so far is only one way in which students can gain contact with the communications environments of other countries. In dramatic contrast is the notion of moving the students bodily to complete part of their studies in another European country. The potential of this has been recognised by the European Community in the form of its ERASMUS programme and in the extension of the principles of ERASMUS, widely perceived as a clear success, to TEMPUS in respect of the former communist countries of Eastern and Central Europe. But what does exchange experience do for the students involved?

As part of a wider study, the authors of this chapter have undertaken research into the aspirations and attitudes of media studies students who have participated in an ERASMUS programme. The data were gathered via a series of in-depth interviews with students who had participated, or were currently participating, in an ERASMUS exchange programme; the forty interviewees were British, French and Belgian.

It is obviously difficult to isolate the precise causal relationship between participation in an ERASMUS exchange and the attitudes and perceptions held by students of European issues and debates. Nevertheless, the following conclusions can be drawn from analyses of interviews.

Many students who take part in European exchanges are already well-travelled, and exposed to a variety of other cultures. For example, over half our UK sample had travelled widely throughout Europe, and to some extent are not typical of the general student population. The ERASMUS programme clearly appeals to those who already have some exposure to different European cultures and knowledge of other countries. Nevertheless, in our study, even the well-travelled report favourably that the exchange scheme increased their awareness of Europe and Europeanism as an issue, and the experience of the exchange made them more aware of media coverage of European issues.

All UK interviewees also believed that their exposure to European media and European media issues broadened and heightened their awareness of the specific features of British media organisations and institutions, and they were now better able to place the latter in an international context. There were, of course, limits to access to cultures that students could generate. For example, UK interviewees were very aware of their language limitations, and expressed the view that students in mainland Europe were more conscious of being part of Europe than they were. Despite this, they did not subscribe to the view that there was a distinctive European culture or a European consciousness, nor did it make sense to talk of a European media; rather, their experiences opened up an interest in different national broadcast systems, particularly the balance between public service and commercial features. The sense of European awareness did not come without particular efforts on the part of students. An important factor in this was a deliberate attempt to mix with other ERASMUS students as well as students in the host institution, and to avoid the temptation of spending too much time with students from one's own country, or even one's own institution.

A major discovery that seems to have taken place amongst students in relation to identification of cultural identity is the realisation that European cultures are identified by their differences and relations to each other. It is not that there is a European culture which can be identified in relation to other cultural identities, but rather there are identities which are constituted only through their relations to each other. Now, whilst this in itself is a significant discovery by students, its implications are limited by the small impact that the ERASMUS experience has had on the curriculum as a whole in Media Studies. Very few students participate in ERASMUS exchange schemes, and many experience problems of re-integration when they return to their host courses, which makes it difficult for them to change the agenda of the curriculum. They are confronted by a majority of staff and fellow-students who have not participated in the scheme, and have not had the same exposure to European issues and European debates first-hand.

Within this broad framework there are differences in the emphases placed on the benefits and drawbacks of a European exchange by students from different member states. UK students placed more emphasis on their growing awareness of Europeanism and European issues than did their counterparts from France or Belgium. They also tended to speak more spontaneously about becoming aware of media coverage of European issues, particularly those relating to other EC countries. Differences in the ideologies and emphases of national education systems are illustrated by the much greater emphasis placed by UK students on their skill development during the exchange period. By this they meant skills developed in taking initiatives, solving problems, managing crises, and in the development of leadership skills. This tended to be coupled with a growing awareness of the importance of self-evaluation, for example asking questions such as 'how am I doing?', 'how am I coping?'

Compared with this, French and Belgian students tended to express a greater concern for trying to understand British media systems as somehow distinct from those they were familiar with in mainland Europe. Whilst they became aware of media coverage of European issues, they tended to see these as being directed by a somewhat insular approach to Europe which saw things European as new, even threatening.

A further difference between UK students and the rest concerned their perception of the curriculum and its emphases. The UK students saw both French and Belgian curricula as having a quite proper concern with communication theory, but often theory for theory's sake which lacked practical application. Some of them saw this as a particularly European trait. This is not to say that British students did no empirical work on the communication and media systems of the region or country in which they stayed. The important factor to note, however, was that the empirical projects they undertook were initiated in the UK, that is, the problems, issues and hypotheses were generated from a UK perspective to be tested out in another European context.

In carrying out their empirical studies, most of the UK respondents gained the impression that relationships between media organisations, practitioners and academics were more fluid and open in Belgium and France than they were in the UK. It proved easier to observe practice and to gain access to organisations than most students had believed, and certainly easier than in the UK. Thus, one element in their perception of being European, or at least being a communication or media student in Europe, was that, despite the emphasis on theory in the curriculum as they perceived it, it was nevertheless possible to undertake close empirical work with media professionals and within media organisations, and thus engage in applied work. By contrast, French and Belgian students made little attempt to undertake this type of work during their exchange period, partly because such projects had not been set for them prior to leaving their host institution, but partly also because they saw less value in applied empirical projects than in exploring theoretical themes and issues in the UK context.

Evidence that there is not yet a European curriculum in communication and media studies is provided by all national groups interviewed in this study. Respondents commented on the difficulty of matching the literature across languages and across national boundaries where problems arose in trying to find equivalents to texts which they had regularly or conventionally used in their host course. To some extent this reflects the different research traditions of mainland Europe and the UK, and the different (but to some degree overlapping) definitions of the subject of communication and media that had developed in these different countries.

There was one respect in which a concern for an interest in Europe as a concept might be seen to be developing, and that was in the work students had done in their host institutions after their European exchange experience. This tended to draw on their growing awareness and knowledge of different national broadcasts and press systems which they began to use with an increased level of confidence. This was particularly true of UK students when they returned to their host courses, but it was not unknown for both French and Belgian students to begin to reflect on theoretical paradigms and the implications that a greater awareness of British broadcast and print media had for their understanding of theory and their ability to utilise it.

A very simple way of putting this is that the exchange period for all students developed at least a degree of curiosity as well as awareness of Europeanism and European issues which will be cashed in different ways when those students return to their host institutions. One must stop short of describing this as a 'road to Damascus' discovery of a world called Europe out there, for it is clear that such dramatic conversions do not take place. However, it would be wrong to understate the increasing awareness of Europe and some of the issues that beset the concept which students develop. It is also important to stress that their incorporation of European issues and the way they utilise them is very dependent on the frameworks and working practices that they have developed in their host courses, and those vary from country to country.

So for the students involved in ERASMUS exchanges it is clear that the effects upon them are significant. ERASMUS makes a real contribution to the way in which communication courses deliver the European mission to their students. But ERASMUS provides for only a minority of students in a minority of institutions. Its ambition is to see 10 per cent of students spending part of their studies abroad and there is no reason to suppose that among communication students the proportion will be very much greater.

The indirect effects of ERASMUS may, however, percolate through to the larger body of students. Previous work by the authors on staff experience of exchanges prior to the existence of ERASMUS showed very important spin-off benefits in terms of encouraging contacts between staff in the collaborating institutions. The consequent networks can, as is shown by this book, be important sources for the development of those supporting materials essential for effective comparative study. But there is an alternative possibility. ERASMUS expects participating institutions to invest the staff time necessary to make exchange partnerships work. It is not too difficult to conceive of a pessimistic scenario in which this burden falls upon the shoulders of those who would otherwise be most concerned with a wider range of co-operation, fatally sapping the energy reserves upon which the broader reform of the curriculum will depend.

NOTE

1 The origins of these are clear in the White Paper: Home Office (1988).

REFERENCES

Blumler, J. (1992) *Television and the Public Interest*, London: Sage.

Home Office (1988) *Broadcasting in the '90s: Competition, Choice and Quality*, Cmnd. 517, London: HMSO.

Langham Brown, J. and Lukyen, G.-M. (1990) *Overcoming Language Barriers in Television: Dubbing and Sub-titling for the European Audience*, Manchester: European Institute for the Media.

UCLES (1990) *International Examination 1990 Advanced Level 9523 Media Studies*, Cambridge: University of Cambridge Local Examination Syndicate.

UCLES (1991) *Examination Syllabus SS21.UK. Media Studies*, Cambridge: University of Cambridge Local Examination Syndicate.

Part II

Chapter 3

Comparing European experiences

David French and Michael Richards

In the chapters which follow this brief overview, examples of the practices of media education in eight European countries are provided. They are explicitly not exhaustive descriptions of all relevant courses in the country concerned. Such directory-like accounts are rarely detailed enough to be interesting and rapidly become out of date.

What the 'national chapters' do offer is a range of experiences of teaching the subject and of course design across a good proportion of the countries of Western Europe. Taken together they show a good deal of similarity and some interesting differences. They provide the source of the themes which are addressed in the rest of the book and indicate some applications of these themes.

By contributing to a shared knowledge of European practices in the field these chapters should help to develop the basis of mutual understanding which will be essential for wider European collaboration. But success in achieving such collaboration will require a familiarity with more than just course content and institutional structures. The chapters range from broad overviews to accounts linked closely to specific teaching materials. This is specifically intended to demonstrate the variety of information that will be required.

All of the national chapters are, in effect, essays in the sociology of knowledge, exploring in different circumstances the processes through which the study of communication and the media has emerged, and the factors which have influenced these processes. The chapter order reflects the different ways this general theme has been approached.

The first four chapters are the closest to broad national accounts. Giglioli's focuses upon the interaction of the highly centralised formal character of the Italian university system and the strong local centres which provide the creative initiatives upon which the development of the study of communication has depended. An important dimension is the link with media institutions, facilitated by the high prestige of Giglioli's department at the University of Bologna.

The core theme of Alvarez's chapter is bound up with the legacy of the Franco dictatorship. Control of the media was crucial to Franco's grip on power and the media have continued to be of central concern in the transition to democracy. Arguably, communication education has a higher profile in Spain than anywhere else in Europe. While in all countries student demand is strong, and several chapters (e.g. Winkin, Giglioli, Gryspeerdt, French and Richards) deal with aspects of the problems and opportunities this offers, no other country counts its communication students in quite so many thousands as does Spain. This intense demand from potential students can be partly attributed to the vigour of the Spanish media.

The system Saeys describes is much smaller, representing only a part of one relatively small country. In Belgium both education and the media have been devolved to become the responsibility of the language communities so that the Dutch-speaking people of Flanders and the francophones of Wallonia each operate their own system. One effect seems, as in Spain, to be a broad recognition of the social and political importance of the media and thus a favourable environment for the growth of media and communication education. Indeed the subject has some of its oldest roots in the two parts of Belgium. One general characteristic which finds particular expression in Saey's chapter is the careful reconciliation of academic and vocational goals, which she neatly characterises as 'knowing why' and 'knowing how'.

The same issue has been central to the British experience, featuring strongly in the chapter by French and Richards. The peculiar institutional division in the British system, which until recently divided higher education into the two sectors of universities and polytechnics, is shown to have had an important impact upon the growth of the subject, leading to a prominent and visible role for education rather than research in the development of the subject and fostering co-operation between colleagues whose disciplinary origins may have been quite disparate.

The next three papers have a more 'micro' approach, with a

heavier emphasis on individual institutions. Winkin, representing francophone Belgium, concentrates upon the tension between forces for change and conservatism in academic institutions. The struggle for recognition for a subject which crosses academic boundaries is illustrated by ethnographic analysis which also provides insight into the power relations between universities and other important cultural institutions.

Eriksson and Heuvelman share a focus upon particular course structures and the factors which have influenced them. Eriksson describes a situation in Sweden in which the subject is now achieving distinctive recognition, while maintaining close links with parent disciplines such as sociology. In common with other relatively small countries, Sweden is very outward-looking, although Eriksson's account raises the interesting phenomenon of a Nordic grouping which must be added, in plotting the cultural geography of the subject, to the more frequently noted French- and English-speaking distinction to which Winkin pointedly refers. Eriksson notes a resolution of 'how and why' questions which parallels that of Saeys, although Sweden seems to have started from a notably more applied position.

The main theme of Heuvelman's contribution is the relationship to the universities of developments in the communication industries. His focus is upon communication management as an emerging field of study and he argues that this should be seen as a response to the increasing managerial complexity of the media in the Netherlands. As the sketch of the particular course at Twente shows, even this overtly vocational concern has required a broad, critical, education alongside elements of narrower technical skilling. Experiences of this kind directly bear out the notion that the demands of theory and practice can be mutually supportive, as is noted in Chapter 14.

Finally, Gryspeerdt, Merten and Barberis address the question of how their courses are informed by intellectual developments in the emerging discipline. In terms of the substance of course content they perhaps offer the closest detail of any of the chapters.

Gryspeerdt, coming from the biggest communication department in Belgium, indeed one of the leaders in the field in Europe, confronts the issue of how the subject is perceived outside the universities and how this perception can impact upon courses. He highlights some of the dangers contingent upon grand generalisations about the ubiquity and importance of 'communication', particularly when these generalisations are often simplistic and inaccurate. A subtitle for his chapter might almost be 'the dangers of misunderstanding McLuhan'.

Merten, in contrast, provides a closely argued exposition of the way in which the assumptions of the study of communication require revision in order to adjust to historical change and theoretical progress. He argues that to construct the subject in terms of the 'media' is to misconstrue the reality of modern communication processes: the clear implication is that education in the field must take a position which locates the media in a wider understanding of communication.

The arguments raised by Gryspeerdt and Merten both inform the reader about the dynamics of intellectual change in their particular countries and raise issues of wider relevance. Barberis has as her concern issues which are more specifically French. Her chapter helps explain why a concern with the detail of verbal and visual language has come to have such a central place in the study of communication in France. Although French work in the field of textual analysis has had an impact across Europe it retains particular prominence in its country of origin and Barberis provides the reader with a direct address to this phenomenon.

As a general representation of the origin and growth of the field in Europe, the national chapters are constrained within the collective experience of the authors. But the coherence of the picture they present is sufficient to imply that it may have wider implications.

The origin of the subject is very clear: its motor force was the recognition of the media as a major cultural and economic form. French and Richards, Giglioli, Winkin, Eriksson, Saeys and Alvarez all deal with this directly. Alvarez's focus upon the transition from dictatorship to democracy contrasts with a more widespread concern with 'media literacy' overlain with a desire to address emerging employment opportunities at a time of expansion in the number of graduates entering the job market.

But if the media provided the initial stimulus, it is clear that there is now a movement towards a broader agenda. Merten provides a theoretical justification for a trend which seems universal, while Winkin provides an extreme example in the 'Anthropology of Communication' programme offered at Liège. Even Gryspeerdt, who warns against the danger of over-extending the field of communication, is really mainly concerned with the risk of it becoming isolated from its foundations in theory and methodology.

The ability of universities to control demand for places to study the subject varies: most systems (see particularly Alvarez, Giglioli and Winkin) provide only limited gate-keeping powers. French and Richards suggest that the highly selective admission process in Britain offers an entrepreneurial opportunity for academic departments to control the direction of development in the subject. A number of authors (Winkin, Saeys, Alvarez, French and Richards) also suggest that the volume of demand has been important in giving particular visibility to teaching and education in the growth of the field.

Perhaps Britain's rather entrepreneurial approach should not be surprising from a country with thirteen years experience of a government ideology which has been aggressively committed to the free market. But Britain is also unusual in the degree of local autonomy allowed to universities in course design and innovation and this is perhaps less to be expected given the centralising trend of British educational policy for younger age groups. Italy represents the extreme of centralisation in university systems, with France not far behind. Elsewhere central political approval for new university courses seems to be the rule rather than the exception, as is shown in the otherwise contrasting experiences of Alvarez, Saeys and Eriksson.

Broadly, the growth of the subject has been from roots in the social sciences (see Giglioli, Saeys, Gryspeerdt, Eriksson, French and Richards). Even where this has not been the case, as in Barberis's account of Montpellier, there are strong links with sociology and contingent disciplines. Of course the range of the social sciences itself provides scope for considerable variation, from Winkin's position, heavily influenced by Erving Goffman, to the more applied concerns of Alvarez.

To some extent, the growth of the field has been facilitated by its ability to 'borrow' cultural capital from the institutions which it studies, as described by Giglioli, Winkin, Alvarez, French and Richards. But it is clear, particularly from Winkin, that such capital does not have a value to academic traditionalists equivalent to that which is at the disposal of the universities.

The authors have generally refrained from speculation about the long-term future. But from their accounts some implications are clear. These are taken up in the final chapter of the book where it is argued that, whatever the vagaries of its development, the study of communication and the media has now arrived as an accepted and increasingly important part of university education.

Chapter 4

Italy
The coming of age of media studies

Pier Paolo Giglioli

The introduction of media studies into higher education has been a long and difficult process all over Europe: a generally conservative academic environment has been reluctant to accept or recognise the credentials of a new scientific field to which it has attributed very little prestige. But the details and the outcome of this process vary quite noticeably in different countries according to the specific configuration of three main variables: the structure of the higher education system and in particular how far it is open to innovation; the relation between the media and intellectuals; and the legal and economic structure of the media systems, especially the relation between the public and private sectors. In dealing with the Italian case, therefore, I shall be concentrating on these three factors.

THE ITALIAN UNIVERSITY SYSTEM: CENTRALISATION, UNDIFFERENTIATED GROWTH AND RESISTANCE TO CHANGE

The Italian university system is one of the clearest examples of centralisation and undifferentiation in the field of higher education (Clark 1977; Giglioli 1979). Formally, the system is strictly controlled from above by the Ministry of Education in Rome and the universities enjoy very little autonomy as far as finance, curricula and selection and management of academic personnel are concerned. The universities are directly financed by the state, which distributes the funds in quite rigid ways according to pre-established categories (normally, there is no chance of transferring funds in the university from one category to another), while the salaries of the academic staff are paid by the Treasury. The curric-

ula are national, the same in each university, and they determine
which components of the student's degree course are mandatory
and which are optional.[1] Only lower level staff are selected locally,
while the higher level posts (associate and full professors) are
allocated through a system of national competitive examinations
held in Rome.

The second structural feature of the Italian university system is
its lack of differentiation. Not only is the private sector virtually
non-existent – the very few private universities are also mostly
financed by the state and anyway have to follow the same rules
as state universities as far as courses and recruitment of academic
staff go – but inside the state sector there is no division of labour
among different kinds of institutions (as, for example, in France
where there is the distinction between universities and *grandes
écoles*): a single organisational structure, the university, must fulfil
the entire range of higher educational functions.

However, the centralised co-ordination of the university system
is more apparent than real. In the first place, the central administrative apparatus is technically weak. Because of the lack of intermediate structures, the formal line of authority between Rome
and the individual universities is thin and feeble; furthermore,
the legal background of Roman bureaucrats makes them more
interested in the formal aspects of the application of laws and
regulations than in the actual overall running of the system.
Second, despite the extremely centralised administration, politicians have never shown the energy and determination necessary
to build up a really *national* higher education system, in which the
local interests of individual universities would be subordinated to
the general interest.[2]

To put it briefly, in practice, the centralisation of the Italian
university system is nominal. The central authority is a kind of
'paper tiger' condemned to issue more and more laws and regulations whose implementation it cannot effectively supervise. In
this power gap academic oligarchies, founded on networks of
informal personal relationships, flourish. The simultaneous existence of these two apparently contrasting structures, personal and
bureaucratic, is not surprising; in fact, the one strengthens the
other and vice versa. The weakness of bureaucratic centralism
facilitates the rise of powerful 'barons' (as the most powerful full
professors are often called in Italy). In turn, individual barons at
the local level or clusters of barons at the national level supply the

main poles of cohesion and co-ordination in an organisation that, because of the split between the centre and the periphery, would otherwise not be easy to govern at all (Giglioli 1979: 41–81).

One of the worst consequences of this intricate interrelation between bureaucratic centralism and personal rule is that the system cannot adequately cope with innovation, growth and change. This was clearly shown by the university system's inadequate response to the challenge of mass higher education. Incapable of differentiation, it reacted to the rapid growth of the student population[3] merely by the swift recruitment of a large number of teachers at the junior levels, which took place mainly in the early 1970s. In purely quantitative terms, the result would seem satisfactory: today there are around 1,200,000 students to 50,000 academic staff, a ratio of 1 to 24. But other figures are much less comforting. For example, the drop-out rate is extremely high: more than one-third of first-year students do not go on to the second year and around one-third of the remaining students do not get their degree in the time normally allotted.[4] These figures show clearly that the growth of teaching staff by itself has not been enough to satisfy the needs of the students, who are not only more numerous than before but often come from lower socio-economic strata and have less solid cultural capital than traditional élite students.

These structural inadequacies have been aggravated by the academic hierarchy's hostility to mass higher education. On the whole, academic staff have shown little or no interest in the needs of the new student population and have calmly gone on doing the same things as before, while the world has been changing rapidly around them. However, business as usual has not been possible after all, if only because the lack of structural differentiation also threatened the traditional functions of the university system, that is, research and preparation for the professions and public administration. Obliged to respond to the new and increasingly varied demands of mass higher education – teacher training, vocational and technological instruction, training for the semi-professions, etc. – the only existing institution, the university, quickly found itself overburdened.

The same mixture of organisational rigidity and resistance to change at the top of the academic hierarchy has characterised the university's response to the establishment of new fields and new subjects, made necessary by a changing and more diversified labour market. Given the existence of national curricula, new subjects cannot be tried out at a local level and, if they turn out to be unsatisfactory, be discarded cheaply; they have to be introduced into the entire system through general regulations. So any proposal to modify the curriculum concerns every university and becomes a critical matter to be agreed upon by both national commissions composed of academics of well-established subjects and ministry bureaucrats, a long and difficult process that can go on for years.

To be sure, in the last few years a limited amount of autonomy and differentiation has been introduced into the university system. For example, shorter vocational courses (three years) have been established, although not yet implemented; individual universities have been granted some autonomy in self-government and accountancy; and a new smaller and more agile Ministry of the Universities and of Scientific Research has been created, separating higher education from the mammoth Ministry of Education. On the whole, however, the general structure of the university system is substantially unchanged. It is in this context that the emergence and institutionalisation of media studies should be considered.

THE EMERGENCE OF MEDIA STUDIES

Television broadcasting started in Italy in the mid–1950s, during a period of great economic development and social change which in the space of a few years transformed a still primarily rural and peasant country into a modern industrialised one. The extent and speed of social and economic change had a deep cultural impact and television played a vital role in this process by exposing a population which had until recently been attached to traditional life styles to new values and to urban ways of life and attitudes. The popularity of the new medium was instantaneous: the number of licence fees grew from 89,000 in 1954 to 1,127,000 in 1958, 3,592,000 in 1962 and 7,000,000 in 1966.

It was at that time that intellectuals began to pay attention to the mass media.[5] As had been already observed (Giglioli 1966; Gundle 1986; Mancini and Wolf 1990), initially this interest had strongly normative and ideological overtones. Both Catholic and leftist intellectuals were convinced that the influence of television was pervasive and they were deeply worried about its effects. But it was on the left that reactions were most hostile and deep anxieties arose over the 'massification' and lowering of cultural standards which it was assumed television would create. Alberto Moravia heavily criticised the advent of an appalling 'second-rate Italy' nourished on a diet of vulgar mass entertainment and banal collective enthusiasms. Pier Paolo Pasolini predicted a sad end to the last vestiges of a genuine popular culture rooted in dialects and local traditions. A well-known journalist, Giorgio Bocca, in a book on the economic boom in Italy, warned that television would rapidly impose dull uniformity over the various regional cultures (Bocca 1963, quoted in Gundle 1986: 577). Of course these anxieties were by no means new: they echoed the most pessimistic predictions of the Frankfurt School, without bothering too much about placing them in an Italian context and without balancing them with recognition of the positive effects of the new medium, for example the contribution it made to the linguistic unification of the country (see De Mauro, 1970).

The reaction of Catholic intellectuals was somewhat different. They did not fear so much that television would degrade high culture, but rather that it would spread individualistic and consumer society values contrasting with traditional Catholic morality.[6] But unlike the leftist intellectuals, the Catholics did not just criticise. Thanks to the control of the Christian Democrats over the public service broadcasting system, they occupied positions of great influence in the RAI (the public service company) and made it into a pillar of rigid morality and an instrument of government propaganda.[7] This naturally strengthened the criticisms of the leftist and liberal intellectuals and added to their alienation from the world of the media.

Only half-way through the 1960s did the cultural debate over television become less ideological and more empirically grounded. This was partly due to the first few studies undertaken by the newly created Audience Research Department of the RAI, whose results introduced greater balance into the discussion of the effects of mass communications. But the most important influence was that of a few sociologists and semiologists[8] who began to take an interest in the media, introducing the American literature on the topic and carrying out the first empirical analyses. Notwithstanding its diffidence towards innovation, the academic world seemed to regard the emerging section without undue hostility, and a small number of experts who did not hold formal university positions were invited to give university lectures on mass communications. Furthermore, a research centre not connected to the university, the Gemelli Institute, was established in Milan and it rapidly became a reference point for psychologists and sociologists interested in analysing the media.

But the unrest of 1968 and its long aftermath in the 1970s interrupted this promising beginning to communication research. In an intellectual and academic environment which had become strongly politicised, empirical research was attacked as an instrument of 'capitalist' science, and even if this attitude was widespread in many sectors of the social sciences, its impact was particularly harmful in an emerging subject such as mass communications. Besides, to many sociologists, media analysis seemed a politically irrelevant and intellectually uninteresting field. Several of those who had started work in the sector abandoned it. The more talented young sociologists opted for sounder specialisations – political sociology, the sociology of work, or social stratification.[9] The result of all this was selective negative recruitment in the field of media studies.

At the same time, achieving full academic recognition of the new subject proved difficult. Those years of great expansion in higher education saw a remarkable growth in sociological subjects in Italian universities, even if this took place in the less prestigious faculties of Education and Political Science, and often in difficult circumstances with quite inadequate structural and financial resources. The new sociology curricula provided for the teaching of mass communications only as single optional courses, and, although the subject was popular among students, not very many universities actually offered such courses: thus, at the start of the 1970s the courses on mass communications held in Italian universities could be counted on the fingers of one hand.

The subject did not even inspire significant research. The main areas of study in the mid-1970s concerned journalism as a profession, the relationship between politics and information and the role of public service broadcasting. But they were approached from a political and ideological point of view, without adequate support from empirical research. For example, serious analysis of the organisation of production was almost completely lacking, and only scant attention was given to audience reception (Mancini and Wolf 1990: 194–6).

The one exception to these negative developments was the

creation in Bologna of a new university curriculum in the field of cultural studies, DAMS (Discipline delle arti, musica e spettacolo), to which I shall now turn.

DAMS: A CASE OF INSTITUTIONAL FAILURE

At the end of the 1960s, some professors at Bologna University proposed the institution of a new curriculum in the area of visual arts, music and the performing arts. The idea was to introduce into the university a series of new subjects (musicology, history and analysis of film and theatre, semiology, mass communications, theory of television language, etc.), and to explore the relationship between high art and popular and commercial art. Because of the proponents' good connections in the ministry and high reputations in the academic oligarchy, the new national curriculum was approved in a surprisingly short time and was operative in Bologna in 1971 (although other universities were thus free to offer the new degree course too, they preferred to wait).

DAMS was innovative not only in its subjects but also in its recruitment of teaching staff. Some of the most important figures on the Italian cultural scene were hired, even if they had but slight connections with the academic world, like Umberto Eco, Furio Colombo (at present Professor of Journalism at Columbia University), Luigi Squarzina (an important theatre director), Luigi Rognoni (an eminent musicologist) and others.

The new degree course, given considerable publicity by the press and immediately a hit with students, could have been an interesting experiment in innovation in the university system. But, because of inadequate institutional protection, it soon found itself in the middle of insuperable difficulties. It formed part of the prestigious but very traditional Faculty of Philosophy and Letters, and was looked upon in a patronising way, if not with downright hostility, by scholars of philosophy or of classical literature, who could not understand how students could waste their time writing theses on soap operas or on pop music; there being no entrance exam, it was soon submerged by a great mass of students, most of whom came from professional secondary schools rather than grammar schools and were none too brilliant; and, more importantly, it had neither enough facilities (libraries and the studio equipment necessary for the new subjects), nor sufficient teaching resources (DAMS students were 50 per cent those of the Faculty of Philosophy and Letters, whereas teaching staff stood at 10 per cent). Finally a series of misunderstandings due to its unclear institutional purposes and relation to the labour market beset DAMS from the start. The students wanted primarily vocational training, to help them become directors, cameramen, television programmers, or musicians. On the other hand, most of the staff were interested in providing critical orientation, not professional instruction. Furthermore, it proved difficult to recruit part-time teachers from the relevant professional sectors (cinema, theatre and television) because they were too busy in their work to be able to teach courses regularly throughout the academic year.

So the DAMS experience ended in failure, generating a good deal of frustration among students and staff. Towards the end of the 1970s and in the early 1980s there were various protests on the part of the students, which culminated in occupations of university buildings; and the staff, although politically leaning mainly towards the left, reacted in a very hostile manner. Since the beginning of the 1980s DAMS has survived only in name as a unified curriculum. It split up into various component parts: a very traditional Department of Musicology and Theatre, a Department of Visual Arts and an Institute of Communication. There is no longer much enthusiasm among the staff and any serious attempt at interdisciplinary teaching is over.

Despite all this, the DAMS experience has not been entirely negative. In the second half of the 1970s it was the main centre for theoretical and empirical research on mass communications and the little group of sociologists, psychologists and semiologists around Umberto Eco has played an important role in giving a new impulse to media studies in the following decade. Besides this, the very failure of DAMS provides us with two important lessons for the future. The first is that, without appropriate entry requirements, the popularity of media studies among students can turn out to be a disadvantage. In the case of DAMS the lack of an entrance exam was clearly fatal almost from the start; the staff found themselves faced by the contradictory need to provide research at a high level, in order to render the subject academically respectable, and simultaneously to invest most of their time in teaching the widest possible range of students.

The second lesson is that the university is not the best place to provide practical training in the media sector, because of the difficulty in finding teaching staff and the lack of the necessary technical equipment. I will return to these two points at the end of the chapter, because they are still relevant to the current media studies situation in Italy.

MEDIA STUDIES IN THE 1980s

The transformation of the media system

The Italian media system changed radically in the 1980s. Following the verdict by the Constitutional Court in 1976, the RAI monopoly of television broadcasting was abolished (apart from news and live programmes, where it lasted until 1990) and the private sector began to expand unchecked by any rules or regulations whatever. The first big private channels were set up in 1980 and after only four years Berlusconi had eliminated his commercial rivals, gaining a virtual monopoly of the private sector and placing the RAI on the defensive.[10]

Berlusconi's strategy developed along two main lines. On the one hand he went for the market demand left unsatisfied by the RAI, that is, pure entertainment. Through aggressive programming of American soap operas, quizzes and talk shows aimed at the weaker points of RAI prime-time scheduling, in a short time he won over a fair share of the public. On the other hand, he built up a solid financial base capturing much of the available advertising revenue left over from RAI (apart from licence fees, RAI is also financed by advertising, although it cannot go over the ceiling established by Parliament to ensure that part of the advertising revenues go to the newspapers).

The RAI counter-attacked, after initial embarrassment, strengthening its subsidiary activities in those areas of the media market adjacent to radio and television broadcasting (records and publishing), investing more in new communication technologies and producing short serials and high-quality films; but above all it entered into the fiercest competition with Berlusconi on his own ground, that of pure entertainment. Overall, even if it has had to restructure its programming, which nevertheless remains basically different from Berlusconi's (Rizza 1989), the RAI has managed to adapt itself to the new market situation and has regained lost ground, without losing too much of its public service image.

The transformation of the radio/television system has markedly influenced both the content and stylistic features of the programmes. In a brief and well-known essay, Eco (1990) contrasted the palaeo-public-service television of the previous decades with the neo-television of the 1980s. And various other observers (e.g. Casetti 1988; Curti 1990; Wolf 1990), although recognising the more negative consequences produced by de-regulation – strip-tease shows, television auction shows and other programmes that in Italy go under the label 'garbage TV' – have noted the modernising effect that privatisation and competition between the various networks has had on television language.

The development of media studies

These changes have modified the relation between the media and intellectuals. The alienation and suspicion of the 1960s and the politicisation of the 1970s have given way to a more pragmatic and precise interest; intellectuals have understood that the problem was not so much to accept or reject mass communications but to understand how they function and to encourage their positive aspects. There are several signs which point to a greater integration between the media and the intelligentsia. For example, some well-known intellectuals write feature articles of television criticism in the newspapers (the most significant example here being that of Beniamino Placido, the television critic of *La Repubblica*, the biggest circulation Italian daily); others collaborate with the RAI (especially with RAI 3, a network somewhat similar to Channel 4 in Britain) or with private channels.

The changed cultural climate has also influenced the academic world, contributing to the development of media studies. The number of individual communication courses taught inside sociology curricula grew slowly during the 1980s and then expanded rapidly at the end of the decade: there were 28 in 1988 and these had grown to 44 by 1991–2. From the point of view of the quality of the teaching staff, the negative consequences of the low prestige of the field in the 1970s have in part continued, especially in the more provincial, outlying universities. But in the first half of the 1980s a new generation of scholars emerged, often trained in the United States, and they have notably raised the level of teaching. Judged on the basis of reading lists and syllabuses, nowadays the theoretical preparation which Italian students receive is not so very different from that which they might get in Britain or the United States. The media sector has also gained more visibility and respectability inside the sociology community. For example, in the Italian Sociological Association, the section on mass communications, created six years ago, is one of the biggest. These clear signs of institutionalisation lead us to believe that the field of media studies has finally come of age. Nevertheless, there are still some problems: here I want to discuss briefly those concerning research and the relationship with the media industry.

Research

The greatest effect that de-regulation has had on media research has been to promote a strong practical orientation. To be sure, for many years the RAI Audience Research Department had been involved in 'administrative research', carrying out inquiries in programme appreciation and into socio-economic features of the audience. But this kind of activity was all part of the RAI's public service mission. In the competitive situation of the 1980s, administrative research became much more clearly market oriented. To get the biggest share of advertising revenues the private channels and also, to a certain extent, the RAI have become obsessed by share ratings and related statistics. So, in addition to Auditel, an agency financed jointly by both sectors to supply non-controversial data on their audiences, a large number of private companies have grown up, especially in Milan, dedicated to pure business research in media matters.

Although some academics have been involved in such activities, on the whole, the university research has remained immune to these tendencies and has maintained its primarily theoretical and speculative character. In general, it has gone in two basic directions. First, research has been concerned with textual analysis of media messages, carried out mainly from a semiotic perspective, which, thanks to the influence of Eco, has acquired a good deal of prestige among researchers. The second, mainly sociological, direction of research concerns themes already dealt with in the previous decade, but treated more empirically and with a sounder methodological base – such subjects as the relation between the media and the public sphere, the problems of radio/television information, the long-term effects of the media, the restructuring of the mass communications system. Recently, ethnographic analysis on reception has been begun, following the work of Morley (1986) and Lull (1982).

Although the quality of these studies has undoubtedly been higher than those of the 1970s, research itself has not been helped by the way media studies have been institutionalised in Italian universities. As I mentioned above, this has happened so far not in the form of an integrated curriculum, but in optional individual courses within the overall degree course in sociology. As a result media scholars are scattered about in various universities and there are no sizeable groups of researchers working in the same place as would be necessary for the functioning of specialised research centres.[11] So research is carried out individually, and there is a lack of collective projects.

In these circumstances the main pole of integration has been supplied by the Programme Analysis Department of the RAI. Created at the end of the 1970s as the research body of the Parliamentary Committee of Control of Public Broadcasting, it has gradually become more and more autonomous, working in close collaboration with academic researchers. It financed most of the academic research carried out in the 1980s and is an important reference point for Italian research workers on the media.

Another obstacle to research is that media scholars are unable to have much say in their own academic reproduction. Since there are no doctorates in communications, media post-doctoral students have to get a degree in semiotics or sociology, and in the national examinations for associate or full professors they are evaluated by semiologists and sociologists not always sympathetic to media studies. So communication researchers, in addition to concentrating on their specific areas of study, have to prove themselves as general semiologists or sociologists, which they often consider a waste of time. The problem, of course, revolves around the issue of whether media studies is an autonomous discipline or simply an interdisciplinary field. Media scholars maintain that what counts as a discipline is determined by the sense of collective identity of its members, by the frequency and intensity of their internal communications and by their being an obviously integrated group to outsiders. Their critics claim that media studies does not have a unified analytical perspective and that a premature separation from the disciplines that have fostered it would be damaging. Both sides have a case and the issue is not easily solved in purely intellectual terms. In the last analysis, as the sociology of science has taught us, these controversies are resolved by organisational factors and power relationships inside the academic world. On this basis, it seems reasonable to assume that the time when media studies will enjoy full autonomy is still a long way off.

The relationship with the media industry

For the successful establishment of a new undergraduate field of study the relationship with the labour market is crucial, especially in a country like Italy which has traditionally had a high rate of intellectual unemployment or underemployment (Barbagli 1974). One of the causes of the failure of DAMS was the lack of clarity concerning what outlets it could offer on the labour market. On the one hand, as I said earlier, DAMS was in no condition to offer practical training to its students. But on the other hand, even if it had done so, the possession of specific technical skills would not have been greatly appreciated on the labour market. In fact, both the RAI (then the only broadcasting industry) and the newspapers preferred to take on graduates with good general qualifications and train them in house for specialised tasks.

Since then, the media world has grown and considerably diversified, especially this last decade. But that has not meant that jobs for graduates have automatically increased. For example, the newspaper industry has become more interested in a better professional preparation of its journalists, but this need has been met by various extra-university schools of journalism,[12] some of which are quite good. Similarly, it is true that the number of television networks has increased (at the moment there are 12 in Italy, 9 private and 3 RAI) and that both Berlusconi and the public service broadcaster commission programmes from outside, thereby stimulating the growth of a market of independent producers. But even here the demand for graduates in communication science has not noticeably increased. For one reason, competition between the two networks has led them to cut expenses and therefore reduce the number of new jobs. For another, in the independent production sector, media students have to face competition from people in the cinema industry (which is in trouble at present) who are generally better qualified for these jobs.

On the whole, the only sector of the labour market which seems promising is that of research, which incidentally is perhaps the only one in which the university can give excellent training. I am not referring so much to the research departments of the RAI and the private networks as to the remarkable number of small and medium sized private agencies specialising in administrative research which have been set up recently. They are most often multi-purpose companies: they work on audience research, as advertising consultants, as opinion pollsters, and they need staff with a good methodological background in the social sciences as well as specialisation in media studies. But here too, although reliable statistics are lacking, the demand for new operators seems limited; that means, considering the popularity of media studies, that a rigorous selection of students for a small number of undergraduate places would be necessary, a measure which is not always easy to carry out in the Italian higher education system.

Future trends: the establishment of a Communication Science curriculum

On 31 October 1991, the Ministry of the Universities and of Scientific Research finally approved a new degree course in Communication Science which was set up in the academic year 1992/3 in six universities: Turin, Bologna, Sienna, Rome, Naples and Salerno. The long process of institutionalisation of media studies in Italian universities would seem to be at an end: from now on, media studies will no longer be taught as individual optional courses in the sociology curriculum, but as an integrated curriculum.[13]

The new curriculum is five years long and consists of a two-year preparatory course followed by three years of specialisation. The first two years aim to give basic courses in sociology, semiotics, public law, communication psychology, communication science, the theory of mass communications, economics and information science. The following three years offers two fields of specialisation, one in mass communications and the other in business communications. The former involves, among others, advanced courses in the sociology of culture, the semiotics of the cinema and television, information and communication law, the theory of radio and television language, the history of the media, methods and techniques of social research, semiotics of the text, the economics and organisation of publishing companies and others. The latter contains courses in business law, company economics, human relations, techniques of advertising communication, public relations and others.

Besides the degree course, two short practical diploma courses of three years' duration have been added, one in journalism and the other in advertising techniques, which both provide for a year of professional training in newspapers and advertising companies.

There is no doubt that, as far as media scholars are concerned, the new curriculum will mean greater social and intellectual integration, helping to overcome the fragmentation that has characterised the field for over twenty years. But as far as students are concerned, it remains to be seen how effectively the curricula will work. Here I would like to make only three points.

In the first place, the curriculum reflects the institutional rigidity of the Italian university system that I have described at the start of this chapter. All the compulsory and optional courses are set out in a national syllabus which is obligatory for every university, whose only freedom lies in choosing which optional courses to offer. Any change in the basic course requires a revision of the national syllabus, which could take years. This, of course, deprives universities of the flexibility necessary to adapt to local circumstances.

The curriculum does, however, have some positive sides to it. For example, the creation of two short diploma courses introduces an important element of differentiation. One may hope that students aiming to obtain mainly practical training will choose the shorter diploma course rather than the full five years. Besides, both short and long courses stress basic training, avoiding premature professionalisation destined to become obsolete in the space of a few years, especially in a rapidly changing technological environment like that of the media.

In terms of job opportunities, in spite of the very optimistic tone of the national committee's report, the new curriculum could create a dangerous surplus of graduates in the media sector. For this reason, all the universities concerned have asked the Ministry to authorise the application of *numerus clausus*. At the time of writing, the Ministry has not replied. The future of the new degree and diploma course will probably be decided on that issue, that is, whether it will turn out to be a successful experiment or whether it will become a sophisticated instrument in training for unemployment.

NOTES

1 A small number of optional courses in the curriculum leading to a degree are determined by the individual universities, but, with this not very important exception, a student working for a degree must take the same courses in any Italian university. As one observer has put it, 'the required courses have been the cement of the [Italian] unitary approach [to higher eduction], the ostensible guarantees of uniformity, the intended reality of the rhetoric that to study law in one place is, in the eyes of the nation, equal to study law in another' (Clark 1977: 54). For the political reasons lying behind the institution of such a centralised and uniform university system, see Giglioli (1979: 9–22).

2 One of the clearest examples of this lack of determination on the part of the political authorities is the failure of the repeated attempts, began during the first years following national unification and continuing throughout fascism, to eliminate a certain number of minor backwoods universities to concentrate financial resources on the bigger or more important ones. However well deserved their suppression, the authorities gave in to local protest. Even after the Second World War, the proliferation of small universities has continued, in opposition to every attempt at the planning or coordination of resources. See Barbagli 1974: 70–80; Caracciolo 1958.

3 The number of students grew from 288,000 in 1961 to 1,000,000 in 1988, and the percentage of the relevant age group going into the universities rose from 7 per cent in 1961 to 30 per cent in 1975.

4 These figures vary significantly across disciplinary fields: in medicine, for instance, the teacher/student ratio is much lower than the average and the freshman drop-out rate is around 15 per cent, while low prestige fields such as sociology, political science and education have a higher teacher/student ratio and a freshman drop-out rate of up to 45 per cent. Of course, the high drop-out rate is a consequence of the fact that in the absence of a university entrance examination – anyone with a high school diploma may enrol – the real student selection takes place between the first and the second year.

5 Because of the strength of its impact, the interest of intellectuals and scholars focused for a long time on television, overlooking the analysis of the social role of the cinema and especially of the radio. Only fairly recently have some historians and scholars of mass communications begun to take up the radio (Cannistraro 1975; Monteleone 1976 and 1979; Isola 1991; Natale 1990).

6 For a summary of Catholic positions on the theme of the mass media in the 1950s, see Gundle (1986: 587–60).

7 Filiberto Guala, the RAI president from 1954 to 1956, when he left it to became a Trappist monk, imposed a severe code of self-censorship on the infant television service, the so-called 'Disciplinary Norms of RAI-TV', which conditioned the character of Italian television for many a year. The RAI's motto, as Bonaventura Tecchi, a Catholic writer and the then president of the committee of control, declared,

should be to 'educate and entertain in moderation', because 'the need to treat moral problems delicately inside the family environment becomes still more necessary than in other situations' (quoted in Mancini and Wolf 1990: 189).

8 Umberto Eco's first book on mass culture, *Apocalittici e integrati*, in which he maintained that ideological and political positions should be accompanied by accurate empirical analysis on the media, was published in 1964.

9 Actually, in the late 1960s the awareness of a crisis in the field of mass communications was widespread not only in Italy, but also in the United States (Tuchman 1988). However, it is interesting to note that while in Italy this led the younger and more politicised generation of sociologists to turn to other fields, in Britain and the USA the opposite happened: many of those at the centre of the renaissance in media studies in the 1970s came from the student movement and the new left. This can partly be explained by the fact that while in Anglo-Saxon countries the protest movements of the late 1960s concentrated mainly on cultural themes, in Italy economic and structural factors were much more important.

10 On Berlusconi's strategy and the RAI's reaction see respectively Schlesinger 1990 and Richeri 1990. On the other important development of the 1980s, the concentration of property in the media field and the birth of multi-media oligopolies, see Giglioli and Mazzoleni (1991) and Mosconi (1992).

11 There are, however, exceptions. The first is the Gemelli Institute in Milan. Set up at the end of the 1960s, it specialised mainly in content analysis (some of it financed by the RAI) and experimental psychological research on reception, understanding and memorising of messages. During the 1970s it was influenced by the growing climate of politicisation and stopped producing empirical research, but it has now gone back to its favourite themes. In Milan there is another lively research group at the Catholic University interested primarily in the semiotic and aesthetic analysis of the media message.

Another important research centre is the Institute of Communication Disciplines, set up on Eco's initiative at Bologna University at the beginning of the 1980s after the DAMS crisis. It works in both mass communications and interpersonal communications and is strongly interdisciplinary in orientation, grouping together semiologists, psychologists and sociologists. At present its main area of research in media studies concerns the semiotics of advertising, political communication, the analysis of television news and the ethnography of reception.

Another small group of researchers exists in the Sociology Department at Rome University and works especially in the field of political communication.

12 Here the RAI is an exception. It has recently set up a school of television journalism in Perugia in close collaboration with the local university.

13 The curriculum, together with the report of the Ministry Commission

which approved it, was published in *Problemi dell'informazione* XVII, March 1992: 17–60.

REFERENCES

Barbagli, M. (1974) *Disoccupazione intellettuale e sistema scolastico in Italia*, Bologna: Il Mulino.

Bocca, G. (1963) *La Scoperta dell'Italia*, Bari: Laterza.

Cannistraro, P. H. (1975) *La fabbrica del consenso: fascismo e mass media*, Bari: Laterza.

Caracciolo, A. (1958) 'Autonomia e centralizzazione degli studi superiori nell'età della destra', *Rassegna Storica del Risorgimento* XIV: 573–603.

Casetti, F. (ed.) (1988). *Tra te e me*, Rome: Eri-Vpt.

Clark, B. (1977) *Academic Power in Italy: Bureaucracy and Oligarchy in a National University System*, Chicago, IL: University of Chicago Press.

Curti, L. (1990) 'Important utopias', in Z. Baranski and R. Lumley (eds) *Culture and Conflict in Post-war Italy*, London: Macmillan, pp. 320–36.

De Mauro, T. (1970) *Storia linguistica dell'Italia unita*, Bari: Laterza.

Eco, U. (1964) *Apocalittici e integrati*, Milan: Bompiani.

—— (1990) 'A guide to the neo-television of the 1980s', in Z. Baranski and R. Lumley (eds) *Culture and Conflict in Post-war Italy*, London: Macmillan, pp. 245–55.

Giglioli, P. P. (1966) 'La sociologia delle comunicazioni di massa in Italia', *Rassegna Italiana di Sociologia* VII: 140–55.

Giglioli, P. P. (1979) *Baroni e burocrati: il cèto accademico italiano*, Bologna: Il Mulino.

Giglioli, P. P. and Mazzoleni, G. (1991) 'Concentration trends in the media', in F. Sabetti and R. Catanzaro (eds) *Italian Politics: A Review*, vol. 5, London: Pinter, pp. 112–25.

Gundle, S. (1986) 'L'americanizzazione del quotidiano: televisione e consumismo nell'Italia degli anni cinquanta', *Quaderni Storici* XXI: 561–94.

Isola, G. (1991) *Abbassa la tua radio per favore*, Firenze: La Nuova Italia.

Lull, J. (1982) 'How families select TV programmes: a mass observational study', *Journal of Broadcasting*, 26(4) (Fall).

Mancini, P. and Wolf, M. (1990) 'Mass-media research in Italy: culture and politics', *European Journal of Communication* V: 187–205.

Monteleone, F. (1976) *La radio italiana nel periodo fascista*, Venice: Marsilio.

—— (1979) *Storia della Rai dagli alleati alla DC: 1944–1954*, Bari: Laterza.

Morley, D. (1986) *Family Television*, London: Comedia.

Mosconi, F. (1992) 'Multimedialità e oligopolio', *Problemi dell'informazione* XVII: 73–103.

Natale, A. L. (1990) *Gli anni della radio (1924–54)*, Naples: Liguori.

Richeri, G. (1990) 'Hard times for public service broadcasting: the RAI in the age of commercial competition', in Z. Baranski and R. Lumley (eds) *Culture and Conflict in Post-war Italy*, London: Macmillan, pp. 256–69.

Rizza, E. (1989), *Costruire palinsesti*, Rome: Eri.

Schlesinger, P. (1990) 'The Berlusconi phenomenon', in Z. Baranski and R. Lumley (eds) *Culture and Conflict in Post-war Italy*, London: Macmillan, pp. 270–85.

Tuchman, G. (1988) 'Mass media institutions', in N. J. Smelser (ed.) *Handbook of Sociology*, London: Sage, pp. 601–26.

Wolf, M, 1989, 'Teorie e metodi nella ricerca italiana sulle comunicazioni di massa', in G. Bechelloni (ed.) *It mutameno culturale in Italia (1945–1985)*, Naples: Liguori, pp. 49–72.

—— (1990) 'The evolution of television language in Italy since deregulation', in Z. Baranski and R. Lumley (eds) *Culture and Conflict in Post-war Italy*, London: Macmillan, pp. 286–94.

Chapter 5

Communication studies in Spain
An individual perspective

Macu Alvarez

At present, the Spanish university system is undergoing a process of reform and renewal of the curricula which make up university degrees. Some of these curricula have now been offered for several decades without modification. Furthermore, the range of the degrees themselves is very limited when compared to that of universities in other countries, a point which is receiving special attention.

When it was passed in 1983, one of the most important goals of the Spanish University Reform Law (LRU) was that of adapting university teaching and degrees to society's present needs in the field of services as well as in industry. The University Advisory Council has already drawn up the general guidelines for all the studies that are to be created or reformed, and the universities were given until 1994 to adjust their degrees to the new plans or add new degrees to those offered at present.

Within this framework, it is almost impossible at this moment to predict what the eventual outcome of the process will be. Each university, within the general rules established, has the independence and authority to draw up a final curriculum for each of the degrees offered as well as to decide the number of years required to complete the degree. The faculties of Information Sciences, created by the General Education Law in 1970, are also affected by these reforms.

It has been sixteen years since the first graduates finished their five-year degrees in Information Sciences in the faculties of Madrid, Barcelona and Navarra, the pioneers in offering this degree. These last two decades have brought about tremendous changes in the practice of these professions and in the means of communication. Not only has the number of mass media changed, but their range of responsibility, ownership models, control and technological level have changed as well. Professional procedures have also been modified; their production methods, sources of information, labour relations, application of the various journalistic genres and even their professional possibilities. But, above all, the concept of what communication and information imply has undergone a profound transformation.

It seems logical that the Information Sciences faculties should have evolved in this same direction, having adjusted their curricula to these developing changes. Nevertheless, this has not been the case.

In Spain, the Information Sciences faculties were founded in the 1970s without ever really being clearly defined. They offered a branch of the Social Sciences degree as an offshoot from the established plan. Later, this took root as an attempt to give greater prestige to journalistic activity. In the early 1980s, these faculties thus urgently and hurriedly met the challenge of the curricula models that are still in effect today.

The 1990s seemed to demand a third phase of communication studies that called for a qualitative change in curricula. This is now being carried out, although some feel that it may be too late. However, a late reply may be valid if it also takes into account other experiences and tries to integrate fully into the European framework to which it belongs. In any case, one must keep in mind the special background of the present-day Spanish state before making judgements; and above all that background which may have directly influenced the development of the Information Sciences faculties which were often considered as of almost equal strategic value to the means of communication themselves, due to the fact that the professionals are and were trained in them.

THE YEARS OF DICTATORSHIP

The most decisive factor in this background is the fact that Spain underwent almost forty years of dictatorship during which the mass media – as well as the profession of journalism – were subjected to appalling state control. The state press strictly followed the government slogans and practice of the profession was subject to obtaining an identity card 'issued' by the state.

According to Alvarez et al.'s arguments (1989), the information policy during the dictatorship was clearly geared to achieving a series of aims, taking into account the validity, importance and possibilities of the mass media. The state demonstrated that it had the power and controlled the staffing of communications enterprises, intervened in the appointment of management, established the norms of the journalistic profession and imposed prior censorship and control of content. Franco was the number one journalist as he occupied the top position in the Registro Oficial de Periodistas (Official Register of Journalists) and the state was the greatest and most powerful employer with the largest mass media empire in Europe.

The totalitarian model was also applied to the training and practical application of the profession. Thus, *La Ley de Prensa* (Press Law) of 1938[1] permitted the Minister of the Interior to regulate the profession, and in article 16 provided for the academic organisation of journalism.

This organisation was formalised in 1941 by a Ministerial Order which created the Official School of Journalists in Madrid. As Pizarroso points out (1989: 243), that school seemed to be modelled after the fascist Scuola de Giornalismo created in Rome in 1930. In 1952, a section of the School was founded in Barcelona and in 1954 a three-year academic diploma course was established.

The Official School of Journalists, which replaced a plan that focused on journalism as a specialised branch of philosophy, had no connection whatsoever with the education or university system. It depended directly on the General Secretary of the Movement (the political organisation of the regime) and, in order to enrol in it, it was compulsory to be a member of the one and only political party. Political services to the regime were considered to be in the applicants' favour, as established in article 9 of the order that created the School (Pizarroso 1989: 243).

Professionals had to enrol in the Official Register of Journalists, mentioned above, by filling out an extremely complicated questionnaire. In this way, and through the action of a judge whose function was to purge the profession, it was possible to know if the applicants were loyal to the 'Fundamental principles of the State', or, in other words, to Franco's regime.

At the end of the 1950s, Catholic groups – such as those described by Pizarroso (1989) – which had been lobbying to obtain their own school of journalism were finally successful and broke the state journalists. In 1958, the Opus Dei set up an Institute of Journalism that was accepted as an official school by the state in

1962. Its graduates had to ratify their academic results through a special examination in the Official School of Journalists. In the same way, graduates of La Escuela de Periodismo de la Iglesia (the Church School of Journalism), founded in 1960 in Madrid, as well as those from La Escuela de Periodismo de la Acción Católica (the Catholic Action School of Journalism), created in Valencia in 1965, had to pass the official examination.

In the late 1960s, an additional year was added to the journalistic studies offered in these official schools, with the objective of differentiating them from lower diploma studies (which at that time lasted three years), but without granting them university status. An Official School of Advertising was set up in Madrid and Barcelona in 1968.

A UNIVERSITY DEGREE

Although professor and journalist Fernando Araujo began a private Journalism course in 1887, moving ahead of almost all the teaching institutions in the world – as Altabella observes (1979: 34) – journalism arrived later than other professions in Spain due to the difficulties involved in its accreditation.

At the end of the last century, almost all of the so-called liberal professions were firmly established in their university-level status and the corresponding degrees were essential to practice. Information Sciences faculties came into existence with the General Education Law of 1970, and in 1971 university studies in Information Sciences began to be offered in public universities in Madrid and Barcelona and in a private university in Navarra.

The Official Schools were discontinued in this way, at a moment when the influence of ideological and political control was diminishing in Spanish society. Nevertheless, as Jones (1992: 150) points out, the arrival of this type of studies in the university was not well received by all the official sectors it was primarily meant to satisfy: the academic and professional sectors. Neither of these groups totally agreed with the proposed aims, the professors chosen to teach the courses or the results obtained.

These first faculties were named Information Sciences faculties, which in itself puzzled and has continued to puzzle students, professors and professionals alike. First, these studies were directed not only to journalists, but also to other professionals in the fields of radio, television, cinema and advertising, not all of whose end products can be considered informative. Second, the concept 'information' has undergone rapid changes and has today taken on other values and connotations.

In this framework, of the public universities, the Complutense University of Madrid and the Autonomous University of Barcelona designed five-year courses for the new faculties, while the University of Navarra did likewise in the private university realm. Madrid began with three fields: Journalism, Visual Image and Audio, and Advertising and Public Relations. Barcelona and Navarra only offered Journalism.

AN AVALANCHE OF STUDENTS

In the 1972/3 academic year, a total of 3,733 students matriculated in the three faculties. This number had almost tripled (9,300 students) by 1975, which was the year the dictator died and coincided with a state of euphoria that filled professionals, company owners and Information Sciences students with hope and illusions. It was expected that the end of the dictatorship would allow greater liberty of expression and inevitably bring about a spectacular increase in newspaper readership.

And the boom did arrive. Six new newspapers were created during the so-called period of political transition: two in the Basque Country (*Deia* and *Egin*); one in Cataluña, with the newspaper *Avui* printed entirely in Catalàn; and three in Madrid – *Diario 16* and *El País*, both of which quickly took a share of the market with the latter becoming a leading newspaper, and *El Imparcial*, which sympathised with the interests of those who had supported the old regime.

These and other newspapers which appeared later required professionals to occupy posts and it was not difficult for the first graduating classes to find a job, as I can well vouch for.

The journalistic profession became fashionable. The means of communication played a key role in Spain during the political transition and the first years of democracy, which resulted in an overwhelming number of matriculations in the Information Sciences faculties. In 1984, 15,049 students were registered, almost 300 per cent more than ten years earlier (see Table 5.1 for a fuller picture).

However, as Moragas's (1982: 574) analyses show, the democratic changes worsened the newspapers' financial problems and the overall number of daily newspaper readers actually dropped.

Table 5.1 Students enrolled in Information Sciences faculties in Spain

1978/9	1981/2	1984/5	1987/8	1990/1	1991/2	1992/3
8,954	8,336	14,748	18,615	23,643	22,960	25,872

Source: State Secretary of Universities and Research and Estadistie National Institute

THE BOOM OF THE MASTERS

In the 1980s the idea that it was possible to learn journalism in one year was strengthened. *El País* started a Master's degree programme in 1986 in its School of Journalism in co-operation with the Autonomous University of Madrid. However, the degree title has no academic value, or recognition: it is an intensive and practical course which is not equivalent to the British MA, for example.

This Master's was and is offered to people with any university degree. The number of students is limited to 32 (a real luxury if we compare this with the massive number of students generally found in the public universities in Spain) and it was anticipated that the high fees would limit the interest shown by the students. However, this was not the case. In the first Master's course (1986), in spite of the fact that there were only 32 places available, more than 800 university graduates sought information about this course and 166 applied for entrance to it. Of those 166, 42.1 per cent already had a degree in Journalism (*Periodistas* 2, February 1987).

The example of *El País* was quickly followed by other news-papers such as *ABC*, *Ya* and *El Correo Español – El Pueblo Vasco* and by radio stations and television channels that created their own Masters or schools to train for the profession.

The philosophy behind these Masters seems to be based on the fact that it is beneficial for the profession to have university level studies because it is practised by university graduates, but that journalistic techniques can be learned in a year and these are based, above all, on practice, the real Achilles' heel of most faculties. Although the budgets for these faculties have increased year after year, which has made it possible to endow them with more facilities, the high number of matriculated students make any facilities insufficient in spite of the *numerus clausus* observed.

The Masters have not been an obstacle to the growth of faculties and in the late 1980s schools were even set up in Salamanca, La Laguna, Sevilla, Valencia and Santiago de Compostela. Apparently, having a university degree in Information Sciences 'helps' one to get a job in spite of the tremendous competition today to secure employment.

THE MARKET REACTION

According to a report for internal use drawn up by the Federation of Press Associations (FAPE) in 1989, professionals in possession of university degrees in Information Sciences, others who come from the old journalism schools and a third group with no specific academic credentials, ranging from lower diploma studies and professionals to university graduates, all co-exist in the journalistic profession.

As this report does not expressly cite the Masters, one can only suppose that the job market has become even more complex due to the appearance of a fourth type of journalist: those who have 'any' university degree and have been trained for a year in the routine production procedures by a newspaper publishing company. That point confirms the almost guild-like concept of practising the profession, which establishes having been trained in a real mini-newsroom with a teacher/student ratio of 1 to 8 and thus having acquired the practical skills needed in journalism as the true system of qualification.

In view of all the classes available to journalists, the job market is experiencing a severe imbalance between supply and demand which has negative repercussions for the Information Sciences faculties' graduates.

The latest available data are taken from a report made by the CEOV – UGT Journalists' Group in 1988 and published in the magazine *Periodistas* (21, April 1989). This study affirmed that 3,500 people were registered in the state unemployment offices waiting for jobs as journalists. Considering that according to FAPE there were 9,000 professionals actually practising at that moment, the conclusion reached was that the number of journalists registered as unemployed represented about 35.7 per cent of that number. In comparison to other university level professions, this percentage is high and is a strong cause for concern.

On the other hand, while the communications industry has experienced almost constant growth, printed periodical information has stabilized or grown very slowly in the last decades. At the moment, the sector is undergoing a crisis that has brought about the closure of newspapers like *El Sol*, *El Independiente* and *Claro* which had been in circulation for two years or less and tried to cater to a nation-wide market.

The sector which has revitalised the job market is the audiovisual field. The job demand for graduates with degrees in Information Sciences has remained stable due to the creation of a greater number of radio stations and the arrival of autonomous and private television stations.[2] One must also bear in mind, however, that a survey carried out recently by the University Advisory Board (*Periodistas* 21, June 1992) affirmed that 23.1 per cent of the Information Sciences graduates working were in posts inferior to their qualifications.

Another alarming piece of information is that unemployment is affecting not only recent graduates seeking their first job, but also journalists who have years of solid experience behind them, and whose newspapers are closing. Meanwhile, the chances of finding a permanent job are increasingly slim. Whereas a few years ago permanent contracts were defended, labour relations have now become more flexible as the legislation follows the European example of giving preference to temporary contracts. Due to the fact that these contracts are limited, the information professional often has to resort to sporadic collaboration through articles, etc., and thus becomes a legally vulnerable entity without the rights that an employee is entitled to in the courts of law.

ACCESS TO THE JOURNALISTIC PROFESSION

In view of this situation, it is hardly surprising that the curricula are being changed in Spanish Information Sciences faculties and that it is also being questioned whether or not it is essential to complete studies in a faculty in order to practise journalism in any of the various means of communication. The subject that is under examination is actually access to the profession itself. Three currents of thought can be said to exist, all of which agree, in general terms, with a survey that the newspaper *El Mundo* carried out in February 1992 among thirty-eight practising professionals. Although percentages cannot be supplied due to the low representative value of the sample and the condensed form of the answers, three groups can be clearly defined. First, it is clear that there are those who firmly believe that the best 'faculties' are the information media themselves, while others are in favour of a university degree as a base, although this need not necessarily be a degree in Information Sciences. The third group believes specific faculties are necessary, provided that they are reformed.

The first group's approach seems quite clear. The journalist is merely an intermediary between sources of information and the public and only needs to learn certain techniques and routine production procedures in order properly to present the message. The second group, who believe any university degree will suffice, feel that completing university studies is essential and seem to favour the fast reprocessing systems offered by newspaper publishing companies.

Those who support the idea of faculties begin by referring to these as 'communication sciences faculties'. These individuals normally have a more global concept of what information and the phenomenon of communications are. They do not feel that it is the university's mission to train information professionals solely to practise a profession based on the apprenticeship of routine production procedures.

The communications phenomenon involves constantly changing and dynamic demands which require professionals who are able to consider communications as a strategic resource in companies or institutions; who can carry out analytic work in the production procedures in the sectors of communications, information and their reception; who are able to design communications policies and show the users how to best utilise the means of communication.

This does not mean that the university must limit its alternatives to the demands of the job market in the industrial sector, which in this case is also subjected to constant technological renovation and the quantitative and qualitative changes this implies. The university cannot be a supermarket; nor should it be governed only by the laws of the market, as Keith Drake, of Manchester University pointed out in the last OECD seminar on superior studies and organised employment (*El País*, 18 June 1992). Nevertheless, the university cannot overlook the fact that the degrees its graduates receive have only relative value on the market. The need for reforms was and is obvious.

STUDENT NUMBERS IN INFORMATION SCIENCES

According to the State Secretary of Universities and Research, 25,872 students matriculated in Information Sciences in the 1991/ 92 academic year. These were students who had passed the university entrance examination, also called the selectivity exam,[3] which determined to a great degree which university studies they could have access to. Almost all the faculties observe *numerus clausus*[4] in an attempt to avoid massive numbers of students which could lead to loss of quality, while at the same time trying to preserve the open character of the Spanish university system.

In order to better appreciate the change of direction these faculties are implementing, it is useful to make a comparison between the present curriculum of the Faculty of Social and Information Sciences of the Basque Country and the new model which has already been approved in the Communications Sciences Faculty of the Autonomous University of Barcelona.

THE UNIVERSITY OF THE BASQUE COUNTRY

The Faculty of Social and Information Sciences of the Basque Country, one of the 297 faculties which exist in Spain, is part of the University of the Basque Country, whose immediate predecessor is the University of Bilbao, founded on 6 June 1968. On 5 February 1980, the University of Bilbao became the University of the Basque Country, thus forming the Public University System of the Autonomous Basque Community financed by the Basque government.

Its oldest teaching centre is the Technical College for Industrial and Telecommunications Engineers, situated in the city of Bilbao and dating back to the turn of the century. The university is spread over three campuses in each of the provinces which make up this community: Alava, Guipuzcoa and Bizkaia.

The Faculty of Social and Information Sciences, set up in 1981, is located on this last campus. Situated approximately 15 kilometres from the capital city of Bizkaia, Bilbao, Journalism and Advertising students share common areas with Fine Arts, Science, Hotel School, Nursing and Medical students. They also share classrooms, student government, the administrative and representative system and leisure-time activities of their faculty with the Social and Political Sciences Branch.[5]

During the 1992/3 academic year, 3,958 students matriculated in Journalism and Advertising. The teaching body is made up of 160 professors most of whom are in their mid-thirties, a relatively young age indicative of, among other factors, the Faculty's recent creation. The body of professors is divided into seven departments and five departmental sections, generally grouped according to areas of knowledge and research.[6]

Students, who are 17 and 18 when they enter the Faculty, begin their first year with Theory and Structure of the Spanish Language, Introduction to Mass Communication, Political Economy, General Sociology, History of Political Thought, Contemporary World History and Structure of Journalistic Reporting. Literature, General Theory of Information, Theory of State and Constitutional Law, and Writing Skills I are introduced in the second year. Technology of the Media, Theory of the Image, General History of Communications and subjects specifically related to the Basque Country – Social Structure of Spain and Euskadi, Spanish Political Law and Basque Autonomous Institutions – are taught in the third year.

In their fourth year, students can then choose between Journalism and Advertising. In the field of Journalism, Mass Communication, Semiotics, Law of Information, Information Agencies, Specialised Journalistic Information, International Relations and History of Social Communication in Spain and Euskadi, in addition to various other subjects, are offered. The major field is backed up by a series of optional subjects that range from Public Opinion to Television News. In the same year the major field of Advertising begins with subjects such as Creativity, Theory and History of Advertising, Marketing I, Motivational Psychology, Research and Commercial Research Statistics. In the final year of their degree, students can choose from optional subjects that range from Public Opinion to News Gathering.

It is important to emphasise that the academic organisation of the current curricula consists of set courses, which form a closed block beginning in October and ending in June. The new plan would attempt to offer greater flexibility throughout the four-month terms, with a credit system and the integration of teaching modules, which would virtually allow the student to draw up the content of his or her own course load.

It is not uncommon for so-called 'practical experience' to be the weak point in an Information Sciences faculty. The profession obviously has a tremendously practical character in which it is continually necessary to repeat routine production patterns. Otherwise, too many points such as, for example, the concept of news would be constantly subjected to re-examination. It is quite difficult to acquire such practical experience anywhere except in a means of communication that is actually in operation, and no matter how many facilities the university may be able to offer, it will always give the impression of being a 'laboratory'.

What the Information Sciences Faculty does ensure is that the student becomes familiarised with computers, practices in radio studios, measures his or her own ability in the photographic laboratory, works on one of the television sets or does research in the phonetics laboratory. Students complain that they receive little practical experience and too few concrete subjects, all of which the new curricula will attempt to rectify by offering more open, less compartmentalised courses where the students themselves can better choose their fields of interest.

EXPLORING OTHER ALTERNATIVES

New initiatives such as a university newspaper published free of charge on a monthly basis, edited in Journalism I by the students themselves and then distributed in the university, are also appearing.

Another very positive experience is that of the junior companies. The only state-wide junior company in the communications and advertising sector is found in Information Sciences and run from the Journalism II Department.

Approximately two hundred students from different courses and major fields are organised in a non-profit-making organisation which is sponsored by the Basque government and the Faculty itself. The company is divided into departments according to fields of interest such as News Gathering, Public Relations, Advertising, Design or Photography, each of which is headed by a student-director. Students acquire self-confidence while putting their knowledge to work carrying out projects for different companies.[7]

In an effort to assimilate communications as a global phenomenon, students make models of magazines and publications, design logotypes and corporate identity manuals for the various compan-

ies, carry out comparative advertising studies and organise conferences like the one held in March 1992 on an 'Analysis of the Last
Ten Years of Creative Advertising in Spain', where attendance
was much greater than they expected.

A professor-tutor coordinates the students' activities, supervises,
orients and helps them to analyse the market conditions, the
effects of the competition and to assess their own professional
practice. Unfortunately, this job is not considered academic and it
receives no official recognition.

What is absolutely clear is that the Information Sciences Faculty
of the Basque Country is receptive to new ideas and eager to
open up co-operation and research lines with other universities
that share these interests. In fact, there is now extensive contact
with Latin American universities and it is quite common for academic staff to exchange experiences, opinions and spend periods
as visiting professors.

Co-operation with European universities is also yielding positive
results. An example of this are the three ERASMUS programmes
now functioning in the Faculty. Student exchange programmes and
visiting professors are thought to be key experiences and the
Faculty actively supports this type of initiative.

THE CURRICULA REFORMS

In March 1992, the Information Sciences Faculty of the Autonomous University of Barcelona's Board of Directors approved the
new curricula as did the Ministry of Science and Education in
January 1993.

The aims of these new curricula range from guaranteeing
specialised theoretical and technical training, so essential for professional practice in the world of information and social communication, to stimulating participation in the creation, development,
transmission and criticism of the communications sciences in the
theoretical and applied fields, and supplying research and analytical background on the different communicative realities.

Three degrees have been introduced – Journalism, Advertising
and Public Relations, and Audiovisual Communication – all of
which may be completed in four academic years divided into two
cycles and organised by four-month terms and credits.

For the Journalism degree, the aim of training 'intellectual
journalists' has been considered foremost together with the defi-

nition of the journalist as a communicator. The academic content of the degree has been divided into four sections: Analysis of Reality (history and social context); Communications Theories and Research, Applied Linguistics, Communicative Production Theories and Techniques (press, radio and television). Analysis of Reality consists of subjects that guarantee the development of the capacity to carry out an adequate interpretation of social reality, concentrating on historical and judicial-political priorities. As these are considered vital to the basic training of a journalist, they are obligatory. Communications Theories and Research determines the nucleus of the specific theoretical endeavour. Applied Linguistics is the basic tool of expression used by the journalistic communicators, and in this sense language plays a role similar to that of mathematics in pure sciences. Finally, Communicative Production Techniques and Theories encompasses the entire range of technological back-up and all the informative genres.

The concrete goals of the new degree in Advertising and Public Relations can be summarised in the following manner:

1 Acquisition of the fundamental theoretical perspectives of advertising communications and public relations, their adjacent or interrelated conceptual bases and scientific areas.
2 Definition of advertising communications' aim, its functions, the scientific fields it influences and those which contribute to fulfilment of its aims.
3 Analysis of specific theoretical bases from the perspective of their relationship with the analysis of the economic and social system which advertising activities and public relations depend on.
4 Knowledge of the techniques and scientific information necessary to solve the problems that arise from the diffusion of advertising messages and the aims of public relations.
5 Study of the effects, quantification, control and evaluation of the efficiency of advertising communications.
6 Acquisition of the theoretical bases and applied interdisciplinary knowledge that furnish a cultural background, considered an essential element in the definition of the advertising and public relations intellectual.

Finally, the Audiovisual Communications degree refers, primarily, to the entire scope of audiovisual production associated with what is popularly defined as fiction and entertainment. Informative audiovisual communications and advertising audiovisual communications receive special attention within the Journalism and Advertising and Public Relations degrees.

This degree is designed around four basic areas of study: Analysis of Social Reality, a series of ten subjects carefully distributed throughout the eight four-month terms of the duration of the degree; Audiovisual Communication: Theories and Research, sixteen subjects mainly studied in the second cycle of the degree; Applied Language and Artistic Expression, seven subjects, studied in both cycles, which deal with the study of the formula and expressive values of oral and written language within the audiovisual, Art, Literature, Music and Design frameworks; Communicative Audiovisual Production Theories and Techniques, made up of a group of twenty-six subjects which must guarantee the interdependence of critical theoretical reflection and concrete experimental knowledge.

A total of sixty subjects which combine sections of theoretical content, enabling the student to undertake analytic and research tasks, with theoretical-experimental teaching sections, to assure rigorous intellectual preparation, make it possible for the students to carry out projects on different levels. These projects mainly deal with script-writing and producing and directing audiovisual and production procedures in entertainment-based radio and television programmes as well as in the cinema and video world.

CONTINUOUS UPDATING

The section which deals with the aims of the curricula in the Information Sciences Faculty of the Autonomous University of Barcelona is extremely important in the Spanish framework. It refers to the fact that one of the objectives of the new curricula is to make it possible for the graduates to receive courses in order to constantly update their knowledge. Until now, postgraduate studies were limited to PhD preparation courses and doctoral theses.

This problem is not unique to the Spanish Information Sciences faculties. According to a reference text handed out in the previously mentioned OECD seminar,

The university has been tremendously affected by the movement related to continuous training, a great part of which has not been assumed. Except in the cases of the USA and Canada, post-graduate training in the member countries of the OECD, in the best of cases, has been under 10%.

(*El País*, 18 June 1992)

Practice of the profession is demanding. Being a journalist, which is what I know best, usually means creating the daily 'story', working against time, rushed by deadlines and, most of all, being in contact with current events twenty-four hours a day.

It is extremely difficult to combine reflection on professional practice with daily practice and updating is sometimes impossible. This is where the university could make a valuable contribution, not only by organising postgraduate courses, but also by putting forth proposals like those contained in this book, which means creating associations to bring together the academic and professional worlds. Both sectors would benefit from closer contact. While academics are sometimes wary of the professionals, and the latter accuse them of analysing reality from isolated positions, they need each other to combine true work conditions and a rational intellectual approach.

SUMMARY AND CONCLUSIONS

Spain has experienced great and obvious change if we take the year 1970 as reference, the year when the subject of Information Sciences was elevated to degree level. Since then, society has evolved and clearly reinforced its decision to live in a democratic system, which guarantees in its Constitution of 1978 freedom of expression, of giving and receiving information. Fifteen years ago, the State had total control of the information services, with authority to regulate the number of communication media, impose censorship, appoint or give the go-ahead to hire staff for these media, and to define the role of the journalist as an apostle of the thoughts and beliefs of the nation. Journalists had to be politically 'examined' to see if they were loyal to the fundamental principles of Franco's regime.

In 1984, Spanish society brought about the division of the State from written forms of communication, and now the same society that relies on a wider range of information calls for a more active role in the communication feedback process. Meanwhile, the faculties of Information Sciences were in great demand. While in 1972 only 3,733 students studied in three faculties, in 1992/3 more than 25,000 students were studying in ten faculties, with little hope of finding a job related to their degree. This evolution in demand, and the impossibility of the job market to absorb it, has put into question the feasibility of these faculties' existence and the method of access to the profession itself.

The degrees offered by these faculties are considered restrictive and rigid, because the professionals needed now are those who use their knowledge as communicators, not only to broadcast information by the traditional means of communication, but also to carry out new tasks with new tools from new social situations. Thus the faculties are re-evaluating the concepts and values on which they were originally based and which determined their character as Information Sciences faculties. They have seen the social demands, analysed the enterprise sector's reply, observed the market tendencies and are evolving into Communication Sciences faculties.

The university should certainly not be governed merely by the laws of the market, but it can influence the job market if it designs its strategies carefully. It can gain an advantageous position if it creates a more polyvalent and flexible type of graduate, and practises its profession according to new demands.

NOTES

1 This law, approved during the Spanish Civil War (1936–1939), remained in effect until it was reformed in 1966 and was not repealed until the present-day constitution was proclaimed in December 1978. Its content was dictated by wartime conditions and provided for rigid control.

2 In three years, the country's situation has changed completely. The original two state television channels have been joined by three private channels and eight autonomous channels, funded by the Autonomous Communities' governing bodies. Spain also has 2,500 radio stations, one of the highest figures in Europe. Spending on advertising has grown spectacularly – by nearly 30 per cent per year during the 1980s – which has contributed to the expansion of the Spanish media.

3 Of the 330,000 students who matriculated in the 1991/2 University Orientation course, figures suggest that some 175,000 passed the examination. This enables them to sit for the selectivity exam, which they must pass in order to apply for pre-registration at university. Acceptance by a university depends on the mark obtained by dividing the sum of the average mark obtained in different sections of the selectivity exam by the personal grade record of the student in his pre-university studies.

4 In the 1992/3 academic year the Information Sciences Faculty of the Basque Country had 760 places available for the first-year university course and required an academic average of 6.64. The Faculty of Sevilla had 460 places available with an average mark of 6.81, and another example, the Faculty of Information Sciences of the Complutense University of Madrid, had 910 places available for Journalism and 310 places for Advertising with a requirement of 6.60.

5 All statistics refer exclusively to the branch of the Information Sciences Faculty: Journalism and Advertising.

6 The departments are: Audiovisual Communications, Constitutional Law and History of Political Theory, International Studies and Political Science, Contemporary History, Sociology and two Journalism departments. Department sections: Political and Administrative Law, Company Law, Applied Economics and Basque and Spanish Philology.

7 The money the companies pay goes directly to the junior company. The money is used to acquire technical equipment, to organise courses for associates or other kinds of activities. Associates pay an inscription fee of 2,000 pesetas and do not receive any economic remuneration. The initiative has been so successful that there is now a waiting list to join the junior company. Entry is restricted for reasons of efficiency and admission is decided solely on a first come first served basis.

REFERENCES

Altabella, J. (1979) 'Breves notas para una historia de la formación del periodista en España', *AEDE* (*Publicación de la Asociación de Editores de Diarios Españoles*), 2, December.

Alvarez, J. T. *et al.* (1989) *Historia de los Medios de Comunicación en España*, Madrid: Ariel Comunicación.

Jones, D. (1992) 'Instituciones que estudian la comunicación en Cataluña', TELOS 30, June.

Moragas, M. (1982) *Sociología de la Comunicación de Masas*, Barcelona: Gustavo Gili.

Pizarroso, A. (1989) 'Política informativa: información v propaganda (1939–1966)', in J. T. Alvarez *et al.*, *Historia de los Medios de Comunicación en España*, Madrid: Ariel Comunicación.

Chapter 6

Theoretical and vocational training in Dutch-speaking Belgium

Frieda Saeys

THE EDUCATIONAL POLICY AS A GENERAL FRAMEWORK

In Flanders, Communication Science and Applied Communication curricula must be situated within the general Belgian policy framework with regard to university and non-university higher education, which has known some remarkable developments over the last decades.

Starting in the 1970s, as a result of constitutional reform, education, which had been a federal matter, was gradually handed over to the communities; this process was completed by 1989. During this period, education ministers of different political orientations came and went, so that within the various communities (Flanders, Wallonia and the German-speaking community) education policies have sometimes shown a lack of continuity ('Onderwijs Belgie' 1984).

Together with this decentralisation, the democratisation of higher education spurred strong institutional growth and an explosion in the numbers of students. In Belgian universities, the student population almost doubled between 1965 and 1977, although since 1977 this growth has begun to slow down (Bragard *et al*, 1982). In the meantime, non-university education of various types and levels began to flourish. In Flanders, co-operation between university and non-university education has been encouraged by the government, which tends to blur the distinction between the two. Nevertheless, the universities remain the prime providers of theoretical curricula, which are complemented to some extent by practice-oriented subjects. Apart from their educational role, universities have an equally important scientific and service-providing mission, which, of course, directly bears on the educational directions chosen.

Another issue is the financing of higher education. This is related to the number of students. Consequently the institutions have a financial interest in attracting as many students as possible. Moreover, there is no *numerus clausus*. The great number and diversity among higher education institutions led to what has been termed a 'school battle'. The phenomenon whereby the various educational networks offer the same service and try to take away one another's students is a well-known tradition in Belgium. This situation came about because of a concern for a number of fundamental human rights (freedom of speech and opinion, freedom of education . . .) but it tends to take on ludicrous proportions. One consequence of all this is an extremely low rate of success among first-year, higher education students, especially at the undergraduate level. Through a decree recently issued by the Flemish government, the universities are required to monitor more closely the progress of their first-year students.[1] However, education and science budgets have been drastically cut back. The same decree provides the universities with a greater autonomy, but has had little effect with respect to another of its objectives, namely the rationalisation of the sector, where fragmentation and cut-throat competition still reign supreme. In order to remain capable of fulfilling its three-fold mission (research, education and service-giving), the universities rely more and more on external financing. Therefore, academic staff must devote a lot of time and energy to management activities as well as the balancing of interests and priorities. On the other hand, non-university higher education's foremost objective is teaching. Financial problems have a direct bearing on student-monitoring activities as well as the purchase of equipment. This clearly teaching-oriented profile, together with generally shorter curriculum lengths, attracts many young people, just out of secondary school or having failed university.

COMMUNICATION SCIENCE AND VOCATIONAL TRAINING

The universities

In Flanders, three universities provide a fully fledged curriculum in Communication Science: KUL (Leuven, Catholic), VUB

(Brussels, non-confessional) and RUG (Ghent, organised by the government). Furthermore, one can follow a partial curriculum at some more recently founded universities (*Marketing Zakboekje* 1990–1: 144–9). This recent fragmentation intensified the competition between the different universities, each one being linked to a well-defined educational network, as they want at all cost to be present in the thriving and supposedly socially important communication sector. In Flanders communication science is a relatively young field. It has developed in a rather pragmatic fashion, depending on the practical possibilities and circumstances within each university. That is the reason why we find communication science within the Faculty of Arts and Philosophy at the Free University of Brussels, within the Faculty of Social Sciences at the Catholic University of Leuven, and, until 1992, within the Faculty of Law at the University of Ghent. In 1992 in the latter university, a Faculty of Political and Social Sciences was founded, where the Communication Science Department is now located.

An important detail is that our discipline has developed in Flanders under the name Press and Communication Science, which the outside world has tended to interpret as a preparation for a journalistic career (*Tien jaar pers – en communicaiewetenschap* 1973). Although primarily designed as scientific, the curriculum appears to have attracted many students whose primary or secondary ambition was to become journalists, especially at the beginning (1960s and 1970s). Currently, as the number of students has enormously increased, there is a corresponding variety of expectations.

This evolution is also due to an increased supply of non-university formal learning opportunities. Until the late 1970s, there was hardly any fully fledged non-university education for professional communicators. The Institute for Journalism in Brussels offered and still offers a professional development course for practising journalists, but this is only taught in the evenings and at weekends. There is also the Arts Academy and the Higher Institute for Theatre and Culture. Nowhere, however, can a fully fledged, specialised journalistic-technical education be found.

Thus many future journalists either study Communication Science or choose another type of general university education (Economics, Philology, etc.). The latter is due to the fact that the media tend to recruit journalists with a general background who may or may not hold a university degree and are not necessarily communication scientists. At the University of Ghent, moreover, the possibility existed for graduate students to obtain in one year a complementary degree in Communication Science, which incited many new students to get another degree first. This 'preferential treatment' regularly caused tensions among the students following the four-year Communication Science curriculum and has now been abandoned by virtue of the Flemish Decree on the universities.

Higher non-university education

In the 1970s the higher institutes for public relations, advertising, journalism and other forms of applied communication emerged. They took advantage of the increasing attention devoted to communication as a sociological phenomenon and underwent an important development stage during the 1980s. The most important educational centres are located in Ghent (HIBO, founded on a private initiative), in Antwerp (provincial institute) and in Kortrijk (institute of the Flemish community). All these curricula evolved from two to three years, which still qualifies as short-cycle education. The institutes of applied communication meet an existing need for a rather practical, short, practice-oriented education expressed by both students and the job market. They also contributed to a better insight into the former complaints and misunderstandings about the lack of practical knowledge and skills of university graduates specialising in Communication Science. It soon became clear that each one of these education levels was able to meet the very diversified, but very real, needs of the professional market.

Know-how or know-why

It is certainly not realistic to standardise all university or non-university curricula. Nor can a strict dividing line be drawn between the two. In order to develop its own identity, to make priorities, to develop a curriculum, to position itself towards the outside world, it is important for a centre to clearly choose to focus on the 'know-how' or on the 'know-why'.

In 1991 the Catholic University of Nijmegen (Netherlands) organised a conference on the theme 'Communication Science in the Nineties'. There seemed to exist a clear consensus that university education has to focus on the 'why' questions. However, this requires technical skills which deal with research design and research method. Involvement of the students in research and the flow of research experience towards education is therefore necessary. This would offer more opportunities for a greater openness and more trust on the part of the media towards the universities in order to work out problems together which lead towards scientific research with a pedagogical dimension. Over the last few years, apart from their thesis, all communication specialists who obtained their degree in Ghent have been involved in at least one major scientific research project in practical circumstances. In collaboration with the NFWO (National Research Council of Belgium) we were able to conduct some major research projects in very close co-operation with both the Flemish and Canadian public broadcasting services. We also participate in internationally designed research on cultural indicators, and we carry out smaller ad hoc studies for the media on a regular basis. We endeavour as much as possible to involve the students in these research activities, as part of their curriculum.

It is true, however, that even though a theoretical education devotes a lot of time to the 'why' questions, one needs to remain fully aware that the majority of the graduates find a job in the 'how' practice. Nevertheless, I do not believe that this is an argument in favour of competing with the more practically oriented education forms outside the university. This has to do with both the interests of the students and the needs of the professional market.

Research

With regard to the specific importance of the theoretical studies as well as research experience, it is easy to recognise that, apart from the increasing recognition of communication as a sociological phenomenon, the research domain has grown bigger and the research questions have become both diversified and more complex. Therefore, one can expect that the need for communication research will only increase. It is the task of the universities to bring good researchers on to the market. It is in the interest of the media and the professional market that the universities have a chance to get sufficient experience in this respect and to transfer it.

Without wanting to make a comparison with the situation in the USA, it is interesting, however, to refer to a research project conducted in 1980–1 by the Ohio State University with students of fifty-four schools of journalism (Peterson 1975). Significant in the results of this research is the fact that even American students of traditional higher institutes for journalism, where the curriculum has long been very practice-oriented, no longer dream about a purely journalistic career. Many are interested in public relations, advertising or all kinds of non-journalistic activities. This does not mean, however, that they also choose institutes which focus on these domains. Among those who choose a journalistic career, the interests are divided among all media sectors (newspapers, magazines, radio, television, photojournalism, etc.). It is remarkable that more than half of the students still do not have any preference during their training. The practice-oriented character of the education does not necessarily make it a direct preparation for professional life. In Holland, the idea that the education of the communicator should focus either on technical education or, with regard to journalism, on background knowledge has been discarded. The professional market's view of that kind of education is not so positive, either, and a lot more attention is paid to qualities such as being able to work independently, adapting to changing situations, working with abstractions, etc.

Such qualities require a specific skill: a good grasp of the communication process as a whole. Therefore, specialisation does not primarily mean the development of any given skill – which may be outdated tomorrow – but the training of different kinds of communicators. In this respect, the Dutch researchers Vos and Van der Wal (1986) emphasise the diversity of qualities which have to be focused on:

• research on the needs of the user;
• attention to the formal aspects of the message;
• easy access to the infrastructure for the user;
• updating the information.

According to Vos and Van der Wal, this presupposes that both generalists and specialists have to be trained. The former must also pay attention to specific problems such as new media and the segmentation of the audience, while the latter need to rely on a sufficiently broad background in order to be flexible.

Finally, it must be clearly stated that the discussion about the theoretical or practice-oriented nature of the media curricula in Flanders is not only related to the specific situation of educational institutions and educational networks, but must also take into account the rights and freedom of the press. One of the most time-honoured points of contact between media training and media practice is journalism, a profession which in Belgium is very profoundly rooted in democratic tradition (Luykx 1978). Any interference with the freedom of the press and the free expression of opinion bears heavy and critical scrutiny from journalists and their professional associations. Therefore, it would be totally impossible to regulate access to the professions which are related to it, through one or another imposed curriculum or degree. In practice, it can be seen, as mentioned above, that neither the print media nor the broadcasting stations require only specific study orientations; instead they need a certain level of general education. The actual training takes place in the workplace. On the other hand, unlike the institutes for applied communication, the universities offer a rather limited number of applied communication courses taught by professional practitioners. The confrontation with practice situations in controlled circumstances is considered to yield interesting elements within a university curriculum, but this may not be allowed to detract from the theoretical orientation, the fundamentally scientific and critical view trained on the media situation.

In Flanders, it seems that the arrival of a commercial television station (VTM) has given a new impulse to scientific communication research. Until 1989, the Flemish media landscape was rather static: a limited amount of newspapers and general information magazines, a non-commercial broadcasting service (radio and television) and a mass of usually commercial local radios. From the point of view of the users, this situation was not generally regarded as limited because of the omnipresence of cable TV.

Television advertising could only reach Flemish viewers through foreign stations, because of an advertising ban in Flanders' public broadcasting service. Since the arrival of VTM in 1989, it was not only the competition for the viewers' attention that heated up: advertising and advertising monopolies became a burning issue, and this not only on a national level but also within the context of European legislation. Research was initiated on various issues, not only for the benefit of the traditional decision-makers (programme-makers, advertising agencies, advertisers, policy-makers) but also on the insistence of new ones such as national and international controlling authorities. In the case of viewer studies, for instance, traditional diary research has been replaced

by audiometry (AGB-system). Furthermore, more and more qualitative research has been initiated: specific research on the attitude
of audience segments, on programme contents, on positioning of
programmes within the total programme supply, etc.

I do not believe that the objective of this book is to open the
debate on the question as to whether the universities should or
should not (and if they should, to what extent) turn to business
sponsorship in general for all their research activities. Nevertheless, we cannot avoid the question as to whether the science of
communication has to focus mainly on research that is financed
in this way, or should formulate and answer research questions of
its own (Van der Linden *et al.* 1991). A discrepancy can originate
between what is socially desirable and what is financially realis-
able. It seems that through the diversification of the media landscape, the multi-mediatisation and the growing impact of the
communication sector on society, there will be an increase not
only in the need for specialised curricula in this sector, but also
in the need for research. Nevertheless, projects financed through
business are still relatively seldom entrusted to universities, so that
the chance that such research might answer burning fundamental
questions as a 'spin-off' (Van der Linden *et al.* 1991) is currently
rather small. I believe that there always needs to be enough room
for truly fundamental research. The amount of money a society is
willing to allocate for this constitutes, in my opinion, an indicator
of the level of civilisation of that society. Furthermore, I think it
is also important that a scientific education offers, sufficiently
integrated general subjects, so that problems are not only
approached from the necessary technical and fragmented point of
view, but are also judged according to their rightful importance in
a broader sociological context.

CASE STUDY: THE COMMUNICATION SCIENCE
CURRICULUM AT RUG (UNIVERSITY OF GHENT)

As an example, let us take a look at Communication Science in
Ghent: we shall describe part of the curriculum and see the way
that curriculum emerged, was evaluated and eventually adapted
and modified, as well as the employment patterns of graduates.
Given the recent spate of austerity measures and the so-called
rationalisation of university education in Flanders, I hardly dare
formulate wishes for the future.

The Master's degree 'Press and Communication' was founded at the University of Ghent in 1962, within the Faculty of Law, on the initiative of a historian, Professor Theo Luykx, who had already been teaching since 1951 an optional course called 'Press Science' (De Bens and Saeys 1989). All these circumstances were not without importance for the development of the curriculum. In the first two undergraduate years, which were common to all political and social sciences students, many historical and law-related subjects were integrated. In the two graduate years and also in the post-graduate course the communication process was methodically approached from different angles (sociologically, psychologically, legally, technically, historically).

In the first years the curriculum had an interdisciplinary character, rather than a well-defined scientific domain with its own object and own method.

Together with the evolution of our discipline in Flanders and abroad, the curriculum had been adapted on a regular basis in Ghent. The most fundamental reform dates back to 1987, when the name 'Communication Science' was introduced. In the four-year cycle the specifically communication-oriented education begins in the second year. The postgraduate course's workload has drastically increased, so that in practice the majority of the students need two years instead of one. During the development of this new curriculum the aim was to strike a balance between the theoretical and practical subjects. All staff members and student representatives were involved in such a fundamental curriculum reform. Their proposals had to be approved by the Faculty Council, where all echelons are represented, and finally by the University's Board of Governors, where, among others, there are representatives of various social, business and political circles. On an informal basis, the programme reform was also thoroughly prepared by means of a questionnaire sent to all graduates for the 1964–84 period. The results were extremely useful as they gave information about the respondents as graduates, job-seekers, employees and, in many cases, employers of new graduates. The results also afforded a view of the diversity of the professional sectors and positions of the respondents, the factors that play a role in recruitment, job satisfaction, etc.

Of course, it is not possible and not even desirable to immediately act on all the shortcomings that may be highlighted by such a questionnaire, yet we must not turn a blind eye to any of them.

Some wishes have since been met, while others are too individual
to warrant action. Moreover, one has to approach carefully any
extrapolation of prognostication in such a fast moving field as
communication. Questioning different classes of graduates gives
an enormous amount of data for fundamental reflection. This is
the reason why a second survey was carried out in 1989. It is our
objective to repeat this on a regular basis in order to catch useful
signals in time.

Some key findings of both surveys[2]

Over the years, student numbers have consistently been increasing.
In the last few years especially, Communication Science has exer-
cised a strong attraction (see Table 6.1).

Table 6.1 Growth in recruitment to Communication Science, University
of Ghent

	1985/6	1986/7	1987/8	1988/9	1989/90
Second-year* undergraduate	–	–	30	41	49
First-year graduate	13	21	27	24	37
Second-year graduate	18	15	22	27	33
Postgraduate	53	55	56	59	75
Total	84	91	135	151	194

* Introduced in academic year 1987/8

Moreover, within the Political and Social Sciences Department,
Communication Science is the most heavily populated section. In
the first twenty-five years during which the University of Ghent
has been offering a (Press and) Communication Science curriculum (1964–1988), 388 students obtained a graduate degree: 172
(44.3 per cent) in the traditional Master's degree programme and
216 (55.7 per cent) in the postgraduate curriculum. (Press and)
Communication Science appears to be predominantly a male
option: in the normal Master's degree curriculum, 53 (30.8 per
cent) women graduated, compared to 119 (69.2 per cent) men. In
postgraduate study also more men than women obtained their
degree: 148 (68.5 per cent) and 68 (31.5 per cent), respectively.
The Communication Science section has clearly been successful.
Over the years, a strong growth of graduates is noticeable (see
Table 6.2).

Of the 388 graduates, we were able to contact 348 in 1989,

Table 6.2 Communication graduates from the University of Ghent

1964–8	21
1969–73	58
1974–8	55
1979–83	95
1984–8	159

sometimes after much research and detection. A total of 243 usable answers came in on time, a response rate of 62.6 per cent, which is almost identical to the 1985 survey response rate (62 per cent). This is certainly a high degree of representativeness, given the fact that characteristics of the respondents differ very little from the distribution of those characteristics among the total population. A total of 174 men (71.6 per cent) and 69 women (28.4 per cent) answered the survey. Among them 143 (58.8 per cent) held a postgraduate degree and 100 (41.2 per cent) had graduated through the normal Master's degree channel. The broad variety of study directions followed by postgraduate students appeared clearly from the answers we received. Graduates of the Faculty of Literature and Philosophy were especially numerous (55.2 per cent) with among them 36.6 per cent of Anglo-Saxon scholars and 18.6 per cent of History specialists. Law students (11 per cent) and Political and Social Sciences graduates (7.6 per cent) were also well represented. The other disciplines (36.2 per cent), although represented by smaller numbers, were very diverse: for example, there was only one Master of dentistry, one veterinary surgeon and one Master of mathematics. The validity of the survey is even reinforced by the fact that the number of graduates and answers received are somewhat parallel over the years.

The objective of the survey was first and foremost to collect data with regard to current job situation, current work conditions and time spent waiting for employment. Furthermore, questions focused on job satisfaction in four domains: level of employment, working atmosphere, working conditions and financial compensation. Among other factors, we tried to evaluate the extent to which previous study directions would have a bearing on the current sector of employment. Details of graduates' paid sidelines were also incorporated in the data.

A first remarkable finding has to do with the diversity of employment. For reasons of consistency, the same categories as in 1985 were maintained with regard to the employment situation

(see Table 6.3). The communication sector remains our graduates'
sector of employment 'par excellence' (33 per cent). Within this
sector, there is nevertheless a wide variety of actual jobs.

Table 6.3 Respondents' distribution within professional sectors, in
percentages

Professional sectors	1985 survey (1964–84 period)	1989 survey (1964–88 period)
Trade and industry	13	20
Communication	35	33
Professional and social organisations	5	5
Education	19	12
Scientific research	3	4
Public administration (BRTN* and education not included)	11	13
Cultural institutions	5	3
Free professions	2	3
Other and miscellaneous	7	6

* Belgische Radio en Televisie, Nederlandstalige Uitzendingen

It is interesting to note that, apart from the print media, many
graduates find work in the audiovisual media sector or in advertising agencies, for instance as copywriters. In strictly non-media
sectors such as trade and industry, public administration and education, there is a recent trend towards more communication-
oriented jobs which may assume many diverse forms. We note
that in these sectors, 55 per cent of the functions occupied by
communication specialists are closely related to communication. In
public administration and in business, according to survey results,
Communication Science graduates take on a new role: that of
communication expert or internal communication officer. Finally,
education, the traditional outlet for Literature and Philosophy
postgraduates, employs fewer graduates (7 per cent fewer than in
the 1964–84 survey). Moreover, in the education sector, there is
more room for specific communication-oriented subjects (8 of the
29 respondents).

Next to the main professional activity, 20 per cent of the respondents have also paid side-activities, the remarkable thing about
this being that they have lately tended to be related to the com-

munication sector (80.8 per cent). For example, an English teacher
might take advantage of his degree in Communication Science by
working as a journalist for a regional newspaper.

The fact that Communication Science as a discipline enjoys
good recognition on the job market is even more obvious if we
look at the short waiting time before employment. For 62.5 per
cent of the graduates the waiting time was less than three months.
Moreover, another 31.2 per cent were able to find a job in less
than one year. Only 6.3 per cent needed more than a year in order
to find a job.

With respect to job satisfaction, one notes that in all professional
sectors the respondents are generally satisfied with their level of
employment: 74.8 per cent are satisfied, 17 per cent are more or
less satisfied, 8.2 per cent are rather dissatisfied. The working
conditions are not a problem either: satisfied (70.5 per cent), more
or less satisfied (23.5 per cent), not satisfied (6 per cent). A large
majority are very positive towards the working atmosphere (80.6
per cent), 15.6 per cent are satisfied, a small percentage are dissatisfied (4.2 per cent). However, the financial compensation appears
to be a sensitive issue in all of the employment sectors: a small
majority (51.6 per cent) are happy with their salaries, 32.3 per
cent are more or less happy in this respect while 16.1 per cent think
they do not earn enough. All in all, the graduates are satisfied
with their jobs. A better financial compensation would perhaps
contribute to even more satisfaction.

It seems that there is a growing interaction between Communication Science as an autonomous discipline and the trend towards
more communication-oriented jobs in professional sectors. Communication Science is not seen by postgraduate students as a mere
appendix to their previous studies. That is why they also create for
themselves more job opportunities in the communication sector.
Moreover, Communication Science graduates must become aware
of the opportunities that are offered to them outside the communication sector, in areas where linguistic knowledge, computer literacy and knowledge of database management can be considered
useful skills. The results of this survey show that one of the factors
that has received attention since the latest curriculum reform, also
at the urgent request of both the students and graduates, is the
link with the diverse opportunities offered by the outside world.

As regards practical experience, an ideal situation would be to
offer a range of possibilities from which students could make up

their own package according to their interests, under the guidance of their professors. This, however, would require the involvement of many external people, which is not feasible financially and practically. Given our existing means, we offer the following:

• a significant number of practitioners;
• a structured training period on a voluntary basis;
• practical assignments related to the lectures.

This relates to both the practical side of research and specific communication skills.

For example, within the course 'Practical Training II' (audiovisual media – 45 hours), students are given the opportunity to choose among three modules from the start of the academic year:

• Within the module 'Journalism', they attend guest lectures and prepare assignments given them by professional broadcasting journalists and follow a training session in a broadcasting corporation or a production house.
• Those who choose to make a video production first follow a technical initiation and are involved in the full production process. The assignments are done for real clients so that students learn to work under production pressure.
• A third group participates in research projects in collaboration with the National Research Council and the Public Broadcasting Service.

In this way, the students are offered the possibility of getting practical, hands-on experience in a structured fashion and from a scientific perspective. The current full curriculum is as follows:

Master's Degree in Mass Communication

First Year

• Logic;
• Law;
• Psychology;
• Philosophy;
• Survey of Belgium's Political and Social History from 1830;
• Contemporary International Political History;
• Sociology;

- Survey of Historical Criticism, applied to Social and Political Institutions;
- Introduction to Social and Political Ideologies;
- The Working of the Mass Media: An Introduction.

Second Year

General courses:

- Economics;
- Information Literacy: (a) Introduction; (b) Applications to Political and Social Sciences;
- Methodology of the Social and Political Sciences;
- Social Psychology.

Courses at the Department of Communication:

- Methodology of Mass Communication Research;
- Survey of the Belgian Press;
- Sources of Mass Communication Research;
- History of the Mass Media (press, radio and television);
- Introduction to Belgian Public Law.

Third Year

- Methodological Problems of Mass Communication Research;
- Study of the Print Media;
- Study of the Audiovisual Media;
- Recent Developments in Communication Technologies and the Media Industry;
- Advertising and Public Relations;
- Marketing;
- Media Law;
- Psychology of Mass Communication.

Fourth Year

- Politics and Mass Media;
- Practical Training I (print media);
- Practical Training II (audiovisual media);
- Exercises in Verbal Communication;
- Study of Copyright;
- Problems in Contemporary Belgian Politics;
- International Economic Institutions;
- Two optional courses (in the third or fourth year).

Postgraduate Course in Media and Communication

- Introduction to Mass Communication;
- History of the Mass Media (press, radio and television);
- Survey of the Belgian Press;
- Methodological Problems of Mass Communication Research;
- Study of Print Media;
- Study of Audiovisual Media;
- Recent Developments in Communication Technologies and the Media Industry;
- Advertising and Public Relations;
- Marketing;
- Media Law;
- Psychology of Mass Communication;
- Study of Copyright;
- Two optional courses.

After a comparative study of the different university curricula in Flanders I came to the conclusion that the reforms introduced in the 1980s have had a diversificatory effect while always taking practical needs into account. More recent developments reaffirm the importance of the fundamental Communication Science in the total package.

Moreover, the above-mentioned Decree (1991) requires the universities to closely monitor their students' workload. Allocating more time to practice-oriented subjects would only be possible at the expense of the fundamental course, which is certainly not a current trend. On the contrary, the specific orientation of the Communication Science curriculum towards the professional world has been emphasised. The fact that job announcements increasingly use the term Communication Science, albeit seldom exclusively, tends to indicate that this policy does have an effect.

Another consequence of the Decree is the new third cycle of study. Ghent was until recently the only Flemish university where one could obtain a Communication Science degree in one year only, even though it had a heavy curriculum and was accessible only to those holding another Master's degree. The new Decree on the universities does not allow this formula. From 1993 on, the one-year Master's degree will be replaced by a third-cycle curriculum (postgraduate), which will be clearly different from the four-year Master's degree (graduate). Other universities offer similar postgraduate programmes. Since it is no longer a basic curriculum, each institution can make up its own the way it sees fit. It is to be expected that there will be a large degree of diversification within these postgraduate curricula. As regards this evolution, the question about the real character of Communication Science as a discipline or an interdisciplinary science is again pertinent.

Right now, in various institutions, people are reflecting on the object and limits of Communication Science, the financing of research, as well as educational objectives and directions. There is a general concern about these problems. Collaboration within the ERASMUS programme offers us the possibility to identify mutual objectives which we cannot realise independently.

NOTES

1 *Decreet van 12 juni 1991 betreffende de universiteiten van de Vlaamse Gemeenschap* (The 12 June 1991 Decree on the universities of the Flemish community).
2 Information in this section is taken from De Bens and Saeys (1989) and Laureys *et al.* (1986–7).

BIBLIOGRAPHY

Bierhof, J. (1986) Conference paper presented at 'Sommatie 1986', Velthoven, the Netherlands).
Bogaert, L. (ed.) (1985) *Informatie-economie: Verslagboek studiedag*, Antwerp: Flanders Technology international.
Bonte, A. (1982) *Werk(-loos): na de universiteit?*, University of Ghent.
Bragard, L. *et al.* (1982) *Les diplômés universitaires belges et leur insertion professionnelle*, University of Liège.
Clausse R. (1971) *Strategie van de communicatiewetenschap: Onderzoek en beleid*, L'enseignement universitaire du journalisme et de la communication sociale, Brussels.
De Bens, E. and Saeys, F. (1989) *Groei en ontwikkeling van de afdeling communicatiewetenschap*, 25 jaar communicatie wetenschap, University of Ghent.
'Enquête bij de studenten in de communicatiewetenschappen, met naschrift van G. Fauconnier (1975) *Communicatie* 5(3): 19–22.
Gids van de Informatiesector (1991) Amsterdam: Strichting Speurwerk.
Huysmans, F. and Van der Linden, C. (eds) (1991) *Communicatiewetenschap in de jaren' 90*, Nijmegen: VSOM.
Laureys, P., Saeys, F. and Verhille, P. (1986–7) '1964–1984: 20 jaar afgestudeerden in de pers- en communicatiewetenschap', *Communicatie* 16(4): 6–10.

Luykx, T. (1978) *Evolutie van de communicatiemedia*, Brussels: Elsevier Sequoia.

Manders, H. and Saarloos, J. (1974) 'Studiemogelijkheden en opleidingen op het vakgebied massacommunicatie in Belgie en Nederland', *Massacommunicatie* 2: 228–43.

Marketing Zakboekje (1990–1) Antwerp: Kluwer.

'Onderwijs België' (1984) in *Winkler Prins Encyclopedisch Supplement*, Amsterdam and Antwerp, 337–40

Peterson, P. (1975) 'Journalistenopleiding in de USA', *Communicatie* 5(2): 20–2.

'Strategie van de communicatiewetenschap' (1973) *Informatiebulletin Cecowe* 3: 18–23.

Tien jaar pers- en communicatiewetenschap (1973) University of Ghent.

Van Cuilenburg, J. (1983) 'Zuinig met, zuinig op informatie', *Massacommunicatie*: 2–14.

Van Cuilenburg, J., Scholten, O. and Noomen, G. W. (1991) *Communicatiewetenschap 1*, Muiderberg: Coutinho.

Van der Linden, D., Huysmans, F. and Mutsaers, W. (1991) 'Communicatie wordt moeilijk wanneer je erover nadenkt', *Massacommunicatie* 4: 326–31.

Vos, M. F. and Van der Wal, G. M. (1986) Paper presented at 'Sommatie 1986', *Massacommunicatie* 2–3: 117.)

Wullaerts, M. (1982–3) 'De arbeidsmarkt voor de Leuvense afgestudeerden in de communicatiewetenschap', *Communicatie* 13(2): 15–16.

Chapter 7

Theory, practice and market forces in Britain
A case of relative autonomy

David French and Michael Richards

British higher education has become increasingly subject to the rhetoric of the market during the Thatcher/Major years. Universities, polytechnics and colleges have seemed ever more open to intervention by business and to the forces of supply and demand, a situation encouraged by a government with an enthusiastic commitment to the commercialisation of cultural life.

The argument of this paper is that British media studies has, in effect, been able to turn these circumstances to its advantage, maintaining a critical, academic, core to its approach by successfully demonstrating that such an informed understanding of communication processes provides its graduates with skills and competences relevant to a wide variety of occupations in the changing media environment.

This situation is given particular appeal by virtue of its resonance with the debate about broadcasting and its relation to the state and capital which took place in Britain during the ten years either side of 1980. That argument, between the professionals' claims of complete independence of the media and the Marxist view of complete subordination, resolved itself in a recognition of 'relative autonomy'. In essence this position accepts that journalists and the ideology of the western media do place great emphasis on independence and on the ability to adopt critical postures towards aspects of the dominant order. Furthermore, such critical scrutiny plays an important part in the operation of modern industrial society, helping to restrain excess, corruption, and to contribute to innovation and the maintenance of the legitimacy of the dominant order. In other words, and to put it simply, if the state wants the benefits of the media it has to accept their relative independence even at the cost of niggling irritations.

In a position of relative autonomy, balance between freedom and restraint is the product of objective conditions and subjective actions. It is our proposition that those involved in British media studies have done a good deal to take charge of their situation and to preserve the space for critical inquiry in the face of material circumstances which at first sight might seem to be difficult to resist.

To understand how this has come about it is first necessary to chart something of the historical context of developments in the educational system in Britain and the place within it of media studies.

THE HIGHER EDUCATION SYSTEM

Background

British higher education has been characterised by a concept known as the binary divide, where higher education has been provided by two types of institution differentially funded with their different histories and different declared purposes: these were the universities, and the polytechnics and colleges.[1] Until the Second World War higher education was provided almost exclusively by the older universities, but since then alternatives have developed. In the late 1940s there was a vast increase in the demand for higher education which the universities were unable to satisfy and many students undertook their studies in technical colleges and similar institutions both for the degrees of the University of London and for higher professional qualifications.

Although new universities had been established in the late 1950s, the student demand for places still outpaced supply and in 1961 the government set up a committee under the chairmanship of Lord Robbins to inquire into higher education. The Committee reported in 1963 and one of its recommendations was that the opportunities for advanced work outside the universities should be extended to degree level. It recommended that the Council for National Academic Awards (CNAA) should be set up. The CNAA became the largest single degree-awarding body in the United Kingdom and one that was to validate the vast proportion of undergraduate courses in Communication Studies, developing as they did in the non-university side of the binary line in British higher education.

In 1967 thirty new polytechnics were created in England and Wales; these were institutions of higher education into which almost three-quarters of the degree work outside the universities was to be concentrated. They were based on colleges of technology, of education and of art and design. The result of all of this was that until 1992 there existed in the United Kingdom a firmly established and recognised system of higher education both inside and outside the university sector. Despite this expansion, access to higher education remained competitive and demand for places outstripped their supply, exceptionally so, perhaps, in the area of communication and media studies.

Recent developments in market forces

The present Conservative government has been committed to the expansion of higher education and increased access to it, resulting in more people having an opportunity to take part in higher education. This later policy of increasing access has been accompanied by a change in funding policies for higher education which has resulted in shifting a significant burden of funding from institutions to students themselves. This means that students now 'carry' increased funding with them, paid by their local education authorities in the main, which they bring in fees to institutions of higher education. Although such funding is often marginal and not related to the full costs of higher education, it nevertheless encourages institutions to expand. Communication and media studies might arguably be able to benefit from this context and expand as a field because the demand for the subject remains high and most communication and media studies courses are relatively cheap to run.

THE DEVELOPMENT OF COMMUNICATION AND MEDIA STUDIES

The creation of research centres in communication studies

A very noticeable feature of the emergence of communication and media studies in British higher education was the distinction between and the difference in location of institutions in which teaching and research took place. The vast majority of undergraduate courses in the field were established in the polytechnics yet the polytechnics were slow to develop postgraduate work and seemed unable to create research centres. By contrast, undergraduate work in communication and media studies was slow to develop in the universities yet major research centres were established during the period following the Second World War. Notable amongst these were the Centre for Mass Communication Research at the University of Leicester, the Centre for Contemporary Cultural Studies at the University of Birmingham and the Television Research Centre at the University of Leeds. In two cases these centres were characterised by significant external funding, in all cases there was a virtually total commitment to research with in some a measure of postgraduate teaching, and all were led by or associated with major figures in communications research in the UK, notable amongst whom were James Halloran, Peter Golding, Graham Murdock, Richard Hoggart, Stuart Hall and Jay Blumler. In all of these cases there was virtually no undergraduate teaching in communication and media studies.

The media industries, education and recruitment

The media industries generally preferred to take responsibility for training of their personnel. The BBC typically recruited Oxbridge graduates and trained them internally for particular professional roles, while independent television companies in turn recruited the same sort of graduate from the BBC. The press, on the other hand, tended to have a preference for non-graduates and recruited people with a view to their being trained through programmes organised by the National Council for the Training of Journalists (NCTJ). There was some limited postgraduate provision in Journalism, notably at City University and University College Cardiff, but these were rare examples in a pattern which tended to give prominence to the recruitment of generalists who were to be trained in-house.

The development of undergraduate courses in communication and media studies

The first wave of undergraduate courses in communication and media studies were established in the 1970s in the polytechnics. They were found in institutions that were geographically scattered across England and Wales; no particular area dominated provision.

Although demand for places on these courses was considerable, the number of places offered tended to be limited to an intake of typically 45 to 50 first-year students, an effect of policies of national funding of higher education which limited the number of students who would be funded in all discipline areas, and communication and media studies was not a favoured area in this respect. The early courses were multi-disciplinary in character, usually drawing on sociology, psychology, literary studies, critical theory and linguistics, and tended to spend some considerable time teaching these disciplines independently before they were to be applied to the analysis of communication institutions and processes. Because of the established nature of training that prevailed in the media professions, these courses avoided any vocational aspirations and offered as their mission media literacy, a critical awareness of the nature of mass media and their practices, an awareness which might have vocational relevance but which was not intended to be a new basis for supplying labour to the media industries. Courses tended to focus on the mass media and mass communication as opposed to inter-personal communication, and gave most prominence to the press, television, film and, to a lesser extent radio. The courses drew upon different national research traditions; thus, for example, psychology was heavily influenced by behavioural approaches well established in the USA, the sociology of the media reflected to some extent the media effects debates developed in the USA post-1940, and cultural studies drew upon the emerging area of British cultural studies which in turn was influenced by the European perspectives of structuralism and semiotics. The CNAA handbook of approved degree courses, which includes a section on 'Communication and Cultural Studies', describes this field as follows:

All of these courses are cross-disciplinary but vary considerably in their content. Most of the Communication Studies courses include some basic studies in sociology, psychology and linguistics. Courses in Cultural Studies investigate the problems of cultural analysis and the relationship between culture and society. Courses in this area may be of relevance to students wishing to work in the media, advertising and the information services, although they should not necessarily be thought of as providing a professional training.

(CNAA 1991)

A second wave of undergraduate courses in communication and media studies began in the early 1980s and this heralded a period of five years or so of growth and change in undergraduate provision. This growth almost doubled the number of courses available from the six or so established in the 1970s, so that by 1987 there were some dozen courses called 'Communication' or 'Media Studies', including the emergence of those described as 'Cultural Studies'. In addition, a new model of course derived from studio-based art and design courses began to emerge. These courses tended to specialise in photography, film and television, dealing with both still and moving images and with an emphasis on practical work. All contained elements of theory, including history of the subject, but a number also offered a broad introduction to subjects such as computer graphics and animation. A significant development in these courses was the greater space given to theoretical and applied studies typical of those which already existed in communication and media studies courses, the effect of which was to narrow the differences between multi-disciplinary communication studies and media studies courses and the studio-based art- and design-derived courses in photography, film and television. A further development during this period was the development of a very small number of professional training courses at postgraduate level, particularly in radio journalism. In addition, during this period the first taught postgraduate courses in communication studies were established. A final feature of the period was the recognition that communication as a set of activities and processes was not exclusively concerned with broadcasting and the press, and a small number of more specialised courses in public relations and marketing, distinct from business studies as a subject, began to emerge. It was perhaps during this period of the 1980s that undergraduate education in communication developed a particular dynamic of its own characterised by an emerging interactive dialogue with the communication industries.

The third phase, from the late 1980s onwards, marked an increase in the provision of undergraduate education in communication and media studies in two specific ways. First, it saw an increase in the provision of modules or pathways in degree course schemes not specifically dedicated to communication or media studies. These were often located in the polytechnics and the colleges of higher education. Communication and media studies became a popular route in combined studies or joint honours schemes. This provision differed from that which had emerged in the late 1970s and early 1980s in that such courses were located in broadly liberal arts, humanities and social science programmes, were theoretical in nature rather than studio-based, and were often taught by staff who were located outside Communication and Media departments who were working in the subject whilst often retaining a foothold in their primary discipline.

The second site of development of undergraduate provision was in the universities. The 1970s and 1980s were marked by very limited undergraduate provision in this area in the universities, the growth and expansion had been primarily in the polytechnics followed by the colleges of higher education. By the second half of the 1980s this situation had begun to change and a number of undergraduate courses were being provided in universities. These courses tended to be theoretical rather than practice-oriented, largely because such institutions did not have the background in art and design education which had produced the studio facilities so necessary for practically oriented courses.

The development of communication and media studies in the school sector

The establishment and expansion of communication and media studies in the school sector closely followed the pattern of the establishment of social sciences in this sector. In a similar fashion to the social sciences, communication and media studies developed as an 'A' level subject variously called 'Communication Studies' or 'Media Studies', and this in turn developed into what were GCE and CSE courses for 15- and 16-year-old pupils. GCE and CSE were subsequently amalgamated into the current award GCSE, and a considerable number of courses in communication, media studies, film, photography and related areas exist at this level. In addition BTEC courses developed in communication and media studies primarily for the further education sector. At the primary level, media studies also finds a place in the National Curriculum, which in the case of English explicitly includes statements about the importance of media education and encourages education for media literacy as a significant part of the teaching of the subject.

There is little doubt that the curriculum for communication and media studies in the school sector has been heavily influenced by curricula in higher education and again this mirrors the pattern of social science. There are perhaps differences in emphasis between the school curriculum in communication and media studies and that in higher education in that greater attention is given in school curricula to work on texts and media products and to the relationships between texts and audiences than is given to aspects of media institutions and media policy.

One of the consequences of the growth of the subject in schools and further education colleges is to add fuel to the demand for higher education in media studies, which since the late 1970s had remained high in any case. This growth in provision also reinforces the recognition of communication and media studies as an appropriate intellectual activity and an area relevant to the future lives of pupils. Nevertheless, the struggle for legitimacy continues in that there is no discrete provision in the National Curriculum for media studies, it is not a core subject, and the body which oversees curricula developments in the school sector, the Schools Examination and Assessment Council (SEAC), does not have a committee for communication and media studies even though a number of courses in the subject exist at primary, GCSE and 'A' levels. The interests of communication and media studies are pursued by ad hoc scrutiny groups or subsumed into the business of the English committee.

SOME QUESTIONS ABOUT THIS HISTORY

For those who have lived and worked through this growth period in the subject, there is a tendency for it to have become 'naturalised', taken for granted. But some episodes are not so straightforward and merit analysis in more detail.

Why did the polytechnics dominate?

It is paradoxical that communication and media studies grew up almost exclusively in the polytechnics rather than in the university sector. After all, the research centres which had given Britain international recognition in the field during the 1960s and 1970s were exclusively in universities. Universities have continued throughout the period to be relatively better funded than the polytechnics and so better able financially to support new fields of study. They also have had the prestige to attract the best minds in those fields which they have chosen to encourage.

In all these ways, the university system was well situated to foster the new subject had it but chosen to do so. The reasons why it did not will become increasingly a matter of historical curiosity if the distinction between polytechnics and universities really disappears following the current reforms. But the history will continue to reveal something about the character of communication and media studies.

Although open to internal debate and a vital source of critical ideas in social and cultural matters, the British university system tends towards tradition and conservatism in respect of new fields of study. It is not entirely coincidental that the successive waves of social science expansion tended to be associated with the emergence of new universities, first red-brick and then concrete and glass, during the twentieth century. In collegiate institutions the recognition of new subjects offers a potential challenge to the precedence of the established disciplines and professors tend not to look enthusiastically on the emergence of new rivals.

Furthermore, the traditional mode of organisation within British universities has been focused on single disciplines. Research centres may be catholic, licensed to draw together expertise from a more diverse range, but departments and undergraduate programmes, despite famous exceptions like 'PPE' at Oxford, tend towards the 'single honours', highly specialised model. Whatever it is now, communication and media studies began as a thoroughly multi-disciplinary activity. As a challenge to academic priorities and assumptions it was less natural as a growth point in the universities than might initially appear.

In contrast the polytechnics had set themselves up with departmental structures which crossed disciplinary boundaries. Economic viability was crucial from the very start and disciplinary units would have been small and expensive. Furthermore, to demonstrate their relevance to modern society and the modern economy (key considerations on the 'public' side of the binary divide), courses and departments tended to be organised around subjects which made sense to the outside world.

These conditions were well suited to the growth of communication and media studies. Claims for the vocational relevance of the subject were often simplistic in the extreme, but were sufficient as tokens to carry conviction in an atmosphere of expansion in which the economic and social importance of the media were increasingly recognised.

Why are there so few taught Master's programmes?

From its slow beginning, communication and media studies has expanded rapidly as an undergraduate subject. But, in comparison with elsewhere in Europe, its growth at the postgraduate level has been slow.

In part this reflects the overall funding situation of British higher education. By international comparison, the per capita support for the living costs of undergraduate students is generous. But the participation rate remains low. All political parties are committed to increasing the proportion of young people in higher education as an important contribution towards modernising the economy and improving international competitiveness. To do so, however, is extremely expensive, particularly if present student support arrangements continue, as seems likely. In these circumstances, it is perhaps not surprising that the expansionary mood does not extend beyond the undergraduate level.

In general, taught postgraduate courses are therefore relatively less common in Britain than elsewhere. They are made less attractive to students by the drastic transition from mandatory financial support, given as of right to all undergraduates (subject to a test of parental income), to the intense competition for the very few grants available for postgraduate study in the social sciences and humanities.

Such sparsity of finance is, in turn, part of a general policy towards the social sciences which has characterised the long period of Conservative government. While one Education Minister who denied the intellectual meaningfulness of 'social science', asserting an inherent contradiction between the two words, has long since passed into retirement, his successors have hardly been more favourable. To them the social sciences, with the possible exception of economics, are crudely linked with socialism and the political opposition. To choose to devote state finance to such activity is inevitably a low priority.

The location of communication and media studies in the polytechnic sector has been an added obstacle to the development of postgraduate provision. The Economic and Social Research Council has only recently begun to direct more than minimal, token, funding beyond the universities. The limited financial resources available to the polytechnics themselves have ensured both that academic course teams would normally devote their hard-pressed efforts to the development of their 'main business', the undergraduate programmes, and such postgraduate courses as have developed have normally been confined to the marginal world of part-time study. These points about taught MA programmes apply with less force to research registrations for MPhil and PhD degrees. The vibrant academic quality of much undergraduate teaching encourages students to step directly into research studentships, although often again carried out part-time.

Why was media studies not absorbed into vocational training?

In these difficult early circumstances, why and how did communication and media studies maintain its critical orientation? Why did it not subordinate itself to the demands of the industry in pursuit of political and institutional acceptance? This is a subject which will be returned to later, as it remains something of a paradox today. But four factors from the early years should be stressed.

First, there is the unattractive nature of the alternative. As noted above, the press and broadcasting in this period had extremely blinkered views about education for their professions. Either they wanted the gifted amateur, open to such in-house training as might be provided, or they desired narrow technical skilling in such matters as shorthand and the structure of local government. A system of higher education which followed this latter model would have had great difficulty in convincing those responsible for monitoring quality that it could achieve so-called 'honours standard'.

Second, there was the nature of the quality control process itself, which was one of peer-review. Those who had to be convinced about the merit of new proposals were other academics and their standards were academic; professionals and representatives of business were either absent or at best marginal.

Third, the nature of the staff involved in course development must be considered. Most were aspirant academics produced by the 'Robbins' experiences of higher education in the 1960s and came from the growth areas of sociology and English literature. Very few had professional experience and as a result the critical faculties nurtured in such backgrounds became dominant in the new field.

Finally, and probably most important, was the intellectual dynamism of research and inquiry in the field. During the 1970s and after, British work in relation to the media and communications achieved international recognition and became a major point of development in the world of the social sciences and humanities. Such excitement in research encouraged and legitimated course designs which themselves attempted to lead students directly to the leading edge of critical, academic inquiry (Boyd-Barrett and Braham 1987).

THEORY AND PRACTICE IN CONTEMPORARY MEDIA STUDIES

During the 1980s the nature of communication and media studies in Britain changed radically and in a way which, towards the end of the decade, positioned it to take a powerful role in controlling its own destiny, despite external pressures.

The conventional indicators of academic vitality suggest a subject undergoing vigorous growth. By the end of the decade categories such as 'communication' and 'media' became prominent features of publishers' catalogues. Not only were books in the field identified as such, rather than being buried in politics, sociology or history, but the simple number of titles had expanded rapidly. But the field had also changed its emphasis. The stress placed in the 1970s on 'critical distance' had been replaced by a growing emphasis on policy, the application to real decision-making of academic ideas.

Originally, the analysis of policy had been an essentially remote activity, considering the ways in which academic theory could expose the limitations of the assumptions made by those taking practical decisions in government or the media industries. When academics devoted their energies to achieving 'real-world' results, the courses which they chose were marginal to the concerns of most practitioners. Such issues as the marginalisation of women and ethnic minorities both in programmes and in programme-making, the cultural closure of the broadcasting élite, the implicit ideological assumptions of the values of news-making, were all far from the centre of the interest of the confident professionals and decision-makers in media organisations. In a way it was 'safe' for critical academics to urge the importance of such topics. If all that could be expected from the practitioners was resistance, then there was no risk of academic purity being undermined by a dangerous, cosy, intimacy with such people. The practitioners could be relied upon to remain behind the bars of their institutional cages, growling occasionally at academic observers when they came within reach.

But, as with so much else in British television, Channel 4 helped to change this. Channel 4 was set up largely to serve groups neglected by mainstream television. In doing so it could be seen as responding to some of the main charges brought against the television establishment by critical researchers.

Of course, this is too simple. Channel 4's mission was primarily determined by the need to minimise competition with established channels. But insofar as Channel 4 could be seen as a response to the academic policy critique, it did demonstrate vividly the relevance of such a critique to the real world of television and its success is further testimony to the accuracy of that critique. The bars had begun to dissolve.

After the experience of Channel 4 and other similar events, mutual confidence between academics and practitioners began to evolve. In particular it became easier, partly because the audience had become more sympathetic, for the academics to demonstrate the vocational relevance of theoretically informed understanding of communication. As this happened, of course, the academics became more interested in devoting time to developing such links.

A relevant example is in the area of audience behaviour. Following the false claim of 'uses and gratifications' (Elliott 1974), the question of what 'watching television' really means became a topic of serious and legitimate academic interest. The processes by which messages are re-interpreted between audience members had long been studied. But now the way that different people behaved in interaction with the screen was the focus (Morley 1986, for example).

The results of the research, showing that people's involvement with television content varies enormously, is clearly of vital interest to schedules, advertisers and others and some of the most interesting work uses effectively collaboration between the industry and the academics. In this situation the old distinction between administrative research, abandoning academic standards for commercial gold, and critical research, which retains academic purity at all costs, becomes less meaningful than ever.

There were a number of other changes which strengthened the 'intellectual negotiating position' of academic media studies. Essentially these were a by-product of process by which the field was broadened and reshaped.

First, the 'target industries' were redefined. Communication and media studies had begun with an overwhelming concentration on the press, broadcasting and film. But graduates from the field got jobs predominantly in advertising, public relations, marketing and kindred areas of business. Furthermore, increasingly analysis revealed the interpenetration of such industries with the traditional media. It would be absurd to begin to discuss the way broadcasting handled the recent British general election without assigning centrality to the promotional techniques, devised from PR and advertising, used by the main parties.

But a crucial characteristic of this wider group of industries is that it had always appeared more receptive to critical analysis than the traditional media. It seemed that the practitioners in such fields more readily saw a relationship between fundamental understanding of communication processes and the ability to innovate and adapt to change.

Not unrelated to this was a redefinition of 'the practical' in media studies. To begin with, practical work had meant the exercise of hands-on skills in media work, particularly with audiovisual technology but also perhaps in journalism. 'Research' had been the stately pursuit of intellectual inquiry. But during the 1980s this changed. Partly as a way of adapting to worsening staff–student ratios without resorting to an unrelenting diet of large lectures, project work, often in groups, became a normal part of student programmes. The subject of such projects were small-scale research topics carried out to tight deadlines. In other words, academic imperatives had redirected student work towards a form which replicated 'practical research' in the media industries, whether programme research for television or market research for advertisers.

This is not to suggest that the courses normally aspired to become pre-professional. The broader range of industries being addressed could make this difficult and, in any case, the original reason precluding such an orientation in the earlier phase still obtained.

The changes noted so far are changes in practical detail and organisation. But they are underpinned by a fundamental ideological change in the self-conception of the academics. Fourteen years of Conservative government, combining the slogans of market freedom with a practice of intensive interference in public bodies, makes academic abstraction difficult. On the one hand, academics have had actively to seek funding for all manner of work from all manner of sources, turning themselves into entrepreneurs in order to do so. On the other hand, some of the broadcasting traditions, such as 'public service', that in more luxurious periods had been treated with extreme scepticism, start to look distinctly more tenable when the alternative is that offered by rampant commercialism. The effect of this is to create a common ground between the practitioners and the academics, in which each can accept as valuable the contribution of the other.

The changes in communication and media studies during the 1980s were accompanied by even greater changes in the media industries themselves.

The rise of Channel 4 has already been noted. Although its audience share remains low (at about 13 per cent) its importance cannot be underestimated. By scheduling programmes it had commissioned, rather than made in-house, it both demonstrated an alternative organisational model and fostered the growth of the independent sector. The two have proved crucial in informing the recent franchise auction which is changing, and will continue to change, the nature of ITV and its output.

But if the new Channel 3 companies will be seeking ratings more vigorously than their predecessors, this is only part of the competition that is building up. BSkyB is now becoming a serious factor and Channel 5 remains available for city television or other uses. Cable is growing slowly but will have increasing importance.

For the BBC the threat is very real. Its position has always depended upon having a major share of audience as well as producing quality programmes. The government has cut back radically on its income and encouraged the adoption of a market model for the internal distribution of resources. Its weakened position will decline further if, as seems probable, its services attract a smaller minority audience share.

In these circumstances, the closed traditions of British television are no longer tenable. New ideas are welcome from wherever they come and bridges can be built between professionals and academics.

How are these changes manifest? The diminished self-confidence of the broadcasters does not imply that the number of job openings in the mainstream media has suddenly increased. Far from it; the recession and the harsh winds of competition have together substantially reduced employment in the BBC and ITV. Even if the competitive chances for communication studies graduates have increased, the competition is much more intense.

But to focus on BBC and ITV/Channel 3 is increasingly misleading. With the rise of the independents, the industry has become more differentiated. Companies may make programmes for broadcasting, advertisements and corporate videos. The turnover of companies in the field is rapid and they can increasingly not be defined by a single media function. Consequently the overall job opportunity range has opened up considerably and the more open attitudes characteristic of, say, PR and advertising have spread back into broadcasting.

The argument so far is grounded largely in experience rather than exhaustive evidence. It could be pushed further into the realm of plausible speculation. The growth of corporate video, for example, suggests an increasing universal concern with communication and the desire to take control of that communication. If that is the case then the market for graduates with broad and flexible competences must be on the increase. If communication and media studies is able to demonstrate that it engenders these competences then its quest for security and a measure of autonomy must become less difficult.

COMMUNICATION AND MEDIA STUDIES AS AN EMERGING DISCIPLINE

The point has repeatedly been made earlier in this chapter that the origins of the field were emphatically multi-disciplinary. Our contention is that it is 'crystallising out' as a single discipline, although we accept that this process still has some distance to go and its final resolution cannot wholly be predicted.

Disciplines are academic collectivities whose members regard each other as their primary professional reference groups. They communicate with each other through books, journals, conferences, research collaborations, etc. They tend to look to each other when job vacancies arise, preferring recruits with a history and/or qualifications in the discipline. Their departments tend to have similar names; external visibility is also manifest in professorial titles.

These features of social organisation are more important than exclusivity or complete coherence of intellectual property. Clearly the discipline has to have a body of ideas which it can call its own but evidence from the natural sciences shows that boundaries are often fuzzy and that similar work frequently goes on in more than one discipline with only minimal cross-recognition.

By these standards, communication and media studies can be seen to be making rapid progress. The number of books coming out makes the field a major section in most current publishers' catalogues. Although the number of journals is still limited, the authors they publish are increasingly from 'within' the discipline and authorities cited by such authors are also mostly insiders.

But there is one important unknown and that is the position of cultural studies. In some British institutions cultural studies fits fairly comfortably within communication and media departments. Its intellectual history has, however, had at some point a significantly different trajectory from our main field and from time to time this has emerged as active conflict. Simultaneously the two have been symbiotic. Cultural studies has been of enormous value to communication and media studies in providing a channel through which ideas from Continental Europe have been introduced to Britain. Communication and media studies, on the other hand, has provided the forum in which 'European' theory can be set alongside that from America and tested against practice.

How this relationship will develop is unclear. Whether the two fields will remain as twin focal points within a single discipline, whether they will wholly merge, or whether they will split, with rival subjects in the forms of the communication and cultural industries, remains to be seen.

Whether the process of achieving disciplinary identity is, or is not, a 'good thing' is a question which defies an absolute answer. Disciplines achieve progress partly by becoming inward looking. The criteria of relevance which they employ enable rapid selection of theories, methods, relevant empirical materials, etc., and little time has to be 'wasted' explaining issues and backgrounds to the non-expert. The only justification for all this is that it 'produces' results. It may be a truism that modern technology is a product of specialists but it is none the less true.

It is, however, worth giving some thought to the contention that the process of 'disciplinary crystallisation' in our field is at a crucial stage, in which it is possible to have some influence over the way in which relevance criteria are defined. Disciplines are in general more or less international. It is particularly important in our field that international links continue to be incorporated as foundations of the discipline.

But less common is the active incorporation of professionals/practitioners within the 'academic' discipline. The bridges between the two groups have, as has been seen, been vital to the successful growth of the subject in Britain. The way in which it defines the memberships of its disciplinary organisations may have a crucial role in determining its long-term identity. However the eventual nature of the discipline is resolved, the process of its emergence is well in train and it will determine the way the field develops and how its members relate to practitioners and to academics in other areas. For example, the increased self-confidence of the academics, frequently noted in this paper, has to be understood in terms of their increased certainty about the coherence and solidity of their own academic identity.

SOME OTHER ASPECTS OF THE FUTURE OF MEDIA STUDIES

What else might the future hold for the development of communication and media studies? We would expect that the emergent relationships with the media and culture industries will be maintained, though not at the expense of the critical independence that has always characterised the subject. The evidence from publishers' catalogues, for example, is that most research and intellectual production is still directed towards a questioning of media practices and their products, coupled, however, with a concern shared with practitioners that threats to cherished values, such as public service broadcasting, must be resisted by media professionals and academics alike.

Developments within education more generally will have their consequences. For example, the general trend towards more modular course structures comprising smaller self-contained units will make aspects of communication and media studies curricula more widely available, but will militate against a further increase in free-standing first degree courses in the subject. We believe that student demand for the subject will remain high and that the increasing emphasis on students bringing funds with them to institutions in the form of higher fees paid ultimately by central government will increase the influence of market forces in deciding which subjects and disciplines will develop and expand in higher education. Communication and media studies is well placed in this respect.

It is likely that postgraduate provision will continue to develop, although lagging behind undergraduate provision in range and provision. Graduates who have followed a free-standing single honours course in communication or media studies are increasingly turning to the MPhil/PhD route as a way of deepening and extending their studies, whereas the taught MA route is becoming established as the conversion route to the subject for graduates who had specialised in other disciplines in their first degree.

Communication and media studies education has not been professionalised, as have some other subjects. There are a few small professional associations which are neither widely used as points of focus for the subject nor sites of significant developments – the exception to this might be The Standing Conference for Cultural, Communication and Media Studies. Similarly academics in communication studies have not yet achieved senior management positions in education institutions outside their immediate departments, and the subject retains a strong grass-roots tradition. Experience from other countries suggests that the recruitment of staff from the field into powerful university positions will mark an important stage in the institutionalisation of the field.

NOTE

1 Although the distinction between universities and polytechnics is important to part of the argument of this chapter, it should be noted that since 1992 polytechnics have been able to apply for a university title and all have done so.

BIBLIOGRAPHY

Alvarado, M. and Boyd-Barrett, O. (eds) (1992) *Media Education: An Introduction*, London: British Film Institute.

Blanchard, S. and Morley, D. (1983) *What's This Channel 4?* London: Comedia.

Blumler, J. G. (ed.) (1983) *Communicating to Voters: The Role of Television in the 1979 European Election*, London: Sage.

Blumler, J. G. and Katz, E. (eds) (1974) *The Uses of Mass Communication*, London: Sage.

Blumler, J. G. and McQuail, D. (1968) *Television in Politics: Its Uses and Influences*, London: Faber.

Boyd-Barrett, O. and Braham, P. (1987) *Media Knowledge and Power*, Milton Keynes: Open University Press.

Briggs, A. (1979) *The History of Broadcasting in the United Kingdom. Vol 4: Sound and Vision*, Oxford: Oxford University Press.

Burns, T. (1977) *BBC: Public Institution and Private World*, London: Macmillan.

CNAA (1979) *The Council: Its Place in British Higher Education*, London: CNAA.

CNAA (1991) *Directory of CNAA First Degree and Undergraduate Courses 1991–92*, London: CNAA.

Elliott, P. (1974) 'Uses and gratifications research: a critique and sociological alternative', in J. G. Blumler and E. Katz (eds) *The Uses of Mass Communication*, London: Sage, pp. 249–68.

Glasgow University Media Group (1976) *Bad News*, London: Routledge & Kegan Paul.

Glasgow University Media Group (1980) *More Bad News*, London: Routledge & Kegan Paul.

Glasgow University Media Group (1985) *War and Peace News*, London: Routledge & Kegan Paul.

Hall, S. (1973) 'The determination of news photographs', in S. Cohen and J. Young (eds) *The Manufacture of News*, London: Constable, pp. 176–90.

—— (1977) 'Culture and the media and ideological effect', in J. Curran, M. Gurevitch and J. Woollacott (eds) *Mass Communication and Society*, London: Edward Arnold.

Hall, S., Hobson, D., Lowe, A. and Willis, P. (eds) (1980) *Culture, Media, Language*, London: Hutchinson.

Hall, S. and Jefferson, T. (1979) *Resistance Through Rituals*, London: Hutchinson.

Halloran, J. D. (1965) *The Effects of Mass Communication*, Leicester: Leicester University Press.

—— (1970) *The Effects of Television*, London: Granada.

Halloran, J. D., Brown, R. L. and Chaney, D. (1970) *Television and Delinquency*, Leicester: Leicester University Press.

Halloran, J. D., Elliott, P. and Murdock, G. (1970) *Communications and Demonstrations*, Harmondsworth: Penguin.

Lazarsfeld, P. (1941) 'Remarks on administrative and critical communications research', *Studies in Philosophy and Social Science* 9: 2–16.

McQuail, D. (1992) *Media Performance: Mass Communication and the Public Interest*, London: Sage.

McQuail, D. and Gurevitch, M. (1974) 'Explaining audience behaviour', in J. G. Blumler and E. Katz (eds) *The Uses of Mass Communication*, London: Sage, pp. 287–301.

Masterman, L. (1985) *Teaching the Media*, London: Comedia.

Morley, D. (1986) *Family Television*, London: Comedia.

Pratt, J. and Burgess, T. (1974) *Polytechnics: A Report*, London: Pitman.

Richards, M. and Withnall, A. (1973) 'Unsure about job prospects: women and the polytechnics', *The Times Higher Educational Supplement*, 2 February, p. 7 .

Robinson, E. (1968) *The New Polytechnics*, London: Cornmarket Press.

Whitburn, J., Mealing, M. and Cox, C. (1976) *People in Polytechnics*, SRHE: University of Surrey.

Chapter 8

When the faculty meets on April Fool's Day
Arts and Sciences of Communication at the University of Liège

Yves Winkin

This chapter is neither a 'defence and illustration' presentation nor a way to deal with local feuds and quarrels. This history of the Department of Communication of the University of Liège is probably an illustration of the ethnographic founding sentence: 'L'universel est au coeur du particulier'. The chapter will attempt to initiate such a move from the token to the type.

It was an odd day, an odd room and an important meeting. The professors of the Faculty of Philosophy and Letters of the University of Liège – a 175-year-old venerable institution – had to approve a boldly original curriculum in Communication, and to decide whether or not three of them were to be suggested to the Board of Administration for promotion as full-time *chargés de cours* (roughly the equivalent of the American 'associate professor'). For months, committees and commissions had met to try to find a consensus on a new programme of courses in Communication. In the early 1990s the Faculty accepted a new programme of *candidature* (roughly the equivalent of the French *DEUG:* the first two years of the undergraduate curriculum) in 'Philosophy and Communication'. The *licence* programme (i.e. the last two years of the undergraduate curriculum) had thus to be modified in order to accommodate the better prepared students (until then, the students only had to have a *candidature* degree in some discipline). So the day had finally come when a vote would cast the fate of the final project and define the career of three academics.

But the day was 1 April 1992, April Fool's Day, which is better respected in Belgium than in many other European countries. Kids try to hang on each other's back a paper cut-out called

April fish (*poisson d'avril*). Adults try to fool a friend with an 'interesting' piece of news. Just about every newspaper tries to fool its readers with a 'very serious' decision by the government; the community-based official radio network (RTBF/BRT) offers phoney formal interviews (e.g. an interview with an alleged representative of NASA, now very sensitive about the Walloon/Flemish issue, in which it has claimed that the next Belgian astronaut was to be Walloon since Dirk Frimout, the first Belgian astronaut, is Flemish).

So the question was: was the meeting the Dean's joke for the day? It was not. The meeting was indeed going to take place. But the meeting room was almost a joke. The Faculty senate room was being painted afresh, so the sixty or so professors were invited to convene in a classroom and to sit in parallel ranks on cramped wooden seats. When they opened the tiny writing tables in front of them, they discovered the latest versions of the love and hate poems students produce year after year. The Dean looked like a schoolteacher asking for some quiet. The blackboard had been poorly cleaned up; spattered chalk covered the floor. Such was the setting of the key Faculty meeting of the year.

The professors apparently loved it. From the start they cracked jokes. It almost looked like the Dean was going to have paper aeroplanes landing on his desk and hear the splat of paper pellets against the blackboard. Yet, in spite (or because) of this slightly surreal atmosphere, the new programme was adopted unanimously in a matter of minutes and the three part-time academics were elevated to full-time positions in less than forty-five minutes. *Du jamais vu.*

Then came the fourth nomination. All of a sudden the mood changed. April Fool was over. The question was: should the Faculty recommend the attribution of two more mass communications courses to a 'practitioner', that is, a media professional invited to the university to share his experience? In the present case, the practitioner was the general administrator of the Belgian, French-speaking, radio and television public network (RTBF) – certainly not a local figure of a small stature, since the RTBF plays a key role in the political, social and cultural life of the country. *Monsieur l'Administrateur Général* had been teaching one media analysis course for many years – but he had no doctorate and no recent publications. Since he already was *chargé de cours* for one course, the extension of his course-load should have been as quick and simple as for his colleagues. But quite a few professors objected to that procedure: their 'colleague' had no doctorate; could not the Department of Communication suggest a doctored scholar for the new courses? The nominee's advocates argued that he was internationally known for his creative work in radio and television programming; that he provided the students with a rather unique insider's view into the media institutions; that he had a keen pedagogical sense and conveyed enthusiasm to his students. No way. He had no doctorate and just a few publications. The debate dragged on. The afternoon was gone (and a good soccer game on television early that evening was getting dangerously near). One by one, professors started to leave the room as inconspicuously as possible. At some point the Dean counted heads: 42 members were needed to cast a valid vote; there were only 38 left. The meeting was adjourned until May. The fate of the media administrator, whose annual budget is twice the size of the university budget, was still undecided.

My decision to focus on a faculty meeting is not motivated by the desire to try to write *à la* David Lodge. That meeting encapsulated twenty years of debates over the profile that the Department of Communication at the University of Liège ought to adopt according to the academics who have been keeping a strong hand over its development throughout the years. A close analysis of local internal politics may reveal patterns which are relevant for much larger concerns. I posit here that ethnography and micro-history may be able to connect that particular case study to general academic trends delineated by sociologists such as Pierre Bourdieu in *Homo Academicus* (1988).

A brief historical sketch is needed at this point.[1]
Oddly enough, the section is still perceived as an incipient department, both inside and outside the University. It was, however, formally established twenty years ago – the initial plans actually date back to the late 1950s. At that time, the idea arose that a 'special school of spoken languages' (*langues vivantes*, as opposed to *langues mortes* such as Greek or Latin) should be created next to the section of Germanic Philology. Languages would have been taught for all practical purposes and professional interpreters and translators would have been trained at the *Ecole spéciale*. The school never materialised as such but a 'Service des

langues vivantes' was created in October 1959 and attached to (but not incorporated within) the Faculty of Philosophy and Letters. Several years went by. The idea of a 'School of translation' was not abandoned but was successively buried in several commission reports. In June 1967, however, the Service des langues vivantes submitted to the Faculty of Philosophy and Letters a bold new programme: a '*licence* in translation sciences' and a '*licence* in public relations'. The argument for the creation of the latter programme is deliciously old-fashioned:

> Persons working in these new communication professions are invested with a huge social responsibility. Yet, almost total lack of specific training necessarily constitutes a heavy handicap for those among such professionals who are in a high-ranking position and want to perform conscientiously and with honour. We feel that such persons must find masters who can assuredly offer them the high level of training they need.
>
> (Internal document, University of Liège)

In early 1968, a common programme of *candidature* was suggested for the two *licences* and a name for the future department appeared: 'Social Communication and Translation.' Yet this was still not the final version of the curriculum. In late 1968, two more projects appeared. One came from the (apparently never discouraged) Service des Langues vivantes, which called for the creation of a 'department dedicated to the linguistic and literary aspects of contemporary European culture'. The expression 'Arts of Speaking' (*Arts de la parole*) popped up, possibly out of the experience of a professor who travelled throughout the United States to gather information (another professor wrote for and received tens of brochures from American departments of journalism, speech, etc.)

The other project came from a 'Development Commission', which was apparently devoted to the production of a global master plan for the entire University. A call was made for the creation of a new unit, whose objective would be

> scientific research and professional training in the field of collective communication. Areas covered under such an umbrella term would be the techniques of translation and interpretation, public relations, newspapers, journalism, cinema, radio, television, theatre, and cultural animation.[2]
>
> (Internal document, University of Liège)

Out of the two projects came a third, with a generic title (*Licence en sciences et arts de la communication*) and three subdivisions (Translation Sciences, Journalism and Public Relations, Performing Arts). Many more meetings and drafts later, a final document appeared in November 1970: Public Relations and Translation Sciences had disappeared; only *information* (i.e. Journalism) and *arts de diffusion* (i.e. Performing Arts) survived. Heavy debates took place at the faculty meeting of February 1971. It was finally decided to screen applicants to the new programme of study through a 'preliminary session' so that the new department would not become 'the refuge of mediocre students, who were unable to complete their coursework in the traditional departments of the university'.

The first preliminary session took place in 1971–2 and the first generation of students was admitted in 1972–3 – on shaky grounds: the University was still not fully committed to maintaining the experimental programme. Still many debates later, the Department was not only maintained but also progressively strengthened, although at a very slow pace. The main steps of that development were as follows:

1976–7

There was a shift from two to four orientations (Press, Television, Theatre, Cultural Animation) and a new emphasis on short training courses offered by professionals from the 'outside world' (mainly journalists) coupled with short work placements (*stages*).

1979–80

The 'preliminary session' was dropped and students with a non-university degree were able to enter directly into the programme, provided that they demonstrated maturity, experience and determination. The channelling was called the 'pink file procedure' – after the colour of the administrative file in which each candidate's application was enclosed – a horrible name, and one that stuck, of course.

1983–4

Five orientations were now offered (Photo-Cinema-Video, Written and Audiovisual Press, Radio and Television, Public Relations and Advertising, Cultural Production and Management); one and a half professors were tenured into the new programme; longer work replacements were required and a third year was offered as a possible way of completing the '*stages*' and the *mémoire*.

1986–9

New orientations were added (Arts and Crafts of the Book, Arts and Sciences of Music). The former five were collapsed into three 'seminars'.

1990–1

The Department was merged with that of Philosophy and a common *candidature* programme in Philosophy and Communication was installed. The success was overwhelming (and the administrative mess was just as great).

1992–3

A new *licence* programme has been launched, with four orientations: Cinema, Media, Music and Anthropology of Communication. As they come out of *candidature* students are offered the choice to pursue their *licence* studies either in Philosophy or in Communication. Three part-time *chargés de cours* have been promoted to full-time *chargés de cours*.

A chronological outline is necessarily tedious: too many facts, too little flesh. Yet quite a few striking elements can be detected.
1 Communication at the University of Liège seems to cover a wide field – probably more than at many other universities, Belgian, European or American. It started with translation sciences and ended up with sciences of music. Orientations were constantly added and dropped, as if the only answer to the first and ultimate question, 'What is communication?', was 'What we put into it'. Indeed, the very many committees and commissions

which kept grinding out notes, memos and projects for more than thirty years never addressed fundamental issues: is there an autonomous discipline called communication? What can we do to contribute to the teaching and research effort in the field? What are the theoretical and methodological options we want to take? Instead, they defined the Department in piecemeal ways, constantly oscillating between a scientific (in fact philological) approach and a professional (if not vocational) approach. As the few excerpts from the reports showed, the programmes were written by academics who only had a vague, naïve and amateurish idea of the realities of the media – and yet could only define the orientations of the new programmes in somehow professional terms (e.g. 'public relations and propaganda') because they did not have command over the realities of the burgeoning academic field of communication either. Thus, a strange hodge-podge of old-fashioned academic and vocational expressions floated around throughout the years. A key explanation of that phenomenon is certainly the intellectual upbringing of the professors who decided over the fate of the new department: most of them were trained as philologists, especially in French medieval philology, and not as social scientists. Very few of them had any knowledge of contemporary research and teaching in communication as provided in American or British universities.

2 The American and British communication traditions were thus never strongly represented in the Department, neither theoretically nor methodologically. As opposed to many European departments, media in Liège were never taught and researched along the lines of Lazarsfeld, Campbell or Gerbner. The canonical American books in the field never showed up on the shelves of the library – they were just alluded to in the mass communication course taught by the top media administrator referred to at the start of this chapter (he spent a few months at Columbia in 1960). The major references were French (Bourdieu, Genette, Metz) or Italian (Eco). British and Australian media and cultural studies were simply unknown to everyone.

It must be said that most professors and students were (and still are) totally incompetent in English – just like in France. Communication departments in French universities also often developed in simple ignorance of the English language, coupled with a vague leftish hostility to the American literature.[3] Empirical research was never valued highly and never carried on in any systematic way. Most valued were philosophical derivations applied to new objects such as the mass consumption society. Until very recently, no thinking was devoted to the basic question 'What is communication?' and no coherent curriculum was implemented to answer it. Most French departments of Communication were built like Liège: with very little money, with people converting willy-nilly at mid-career, and with many students coming out of everywhere aspiring to become 'journalists'.

3 The reference to journalism is a constant feature of the Department. All of the many projects, either killed before Faculty approval or actually voted and turned into curricula, included courses on the press rather than the media. Two kinds of courses were constantly reinvented: theoretical and practical courses. The first kind included courses such as the history of Belgian newspapers, and the critical analysis of news; the second comprised a few short courses offered by actual journalists and a few weeks of work placement in a local newspaper or at the RTBF station in Liège. As a professional training, it was a joke (as compared to American schools of journalism, for example, or even to the Ecole de Journalisme of Lille, in France). But there was no way this pseudo-training could ever be called into question and – *horresco referens* – phased out. It was (and still is) symbolically (for others strategically) necessary to ground the Department in some reality – or rather into a well-shared illusion: namely that a communication department produces professionals, that is, journalists, television producers – if not PR officers. For people outside the discipline (either parents, educators or professors of the Faculty of Philosophy and Letters who decide over the fate of the Department), communication did (and still does) not exist as a scholarly discipline, producing its own issues like any other discipline. It is not established in such a way yet. Communication still needs a professional goal as its *raison d'être*. Journalism is convenient enough: everybody knows what a journalist does.

The debate between academics and practitioners thus never took place either inside or outside the Department. The necessity of training was never questioned: professional courses and work placements were included in the many variants of the curriculum over the years. Yet it was also very clear that academic courses were to predominate. Practitioners never got the chance to argue for a real professional curriculum, with a few academic courses appended, that is, a curriculum which would be the symmetrical inversion of the traditional distribution of courses. They never had anything to say in a decision-making committee; they always came and went, as honourable guests of the University. So long as they behaved as polite outsiders, they were most welcome. Surprisingly, the media professionals never retaliated. For a few years, local journalists, who usually had no university degree, complained bitterly abut the '8th section' students. But they never turned their criticisms into a memorandum, for example, calling for a better media education. They never mounted a media campaign against the Department. They mainly harassed the new summer students on work placements for a few days, showing them they did not learn anything useful at the University since they did not even learn how to type. Actually the local newspapers behaved like parents, awed yet unthreatened by their children's nearly acquired competencies when they try to compete with them on their own ground.

4 Theatre, cultural animation, public relations, advertising, book publishing, cultural production and management, even music, all matters which kept appearing and disappearing in the multiple programmes, were justified on professional grounds as well. The job market apparently needed such professionals and the Department of Communication had to address such demands through new courses and invitations to PR officers, publishers, cultural producers and managers to come and teach their art and experience. All of those people not only gave an *éclat* to the Department; they also reinforced its very necessity. Yet all of them were always marginal in the decision processes, in terms of curriculum changes, jury deliberations or allocations of credits. The inner core of the Department was made of the permanent staff, whose own teaching had nothing to do with professional training.

It is all the more surprising in that respect to observe the recent creation of a new course orientation called Anthropology of Communication, which makes no claim for professional relevance. It was pushed forward by a junior Faculty member who made a career out of importing American ideas about interpersonal communication. Long protected by a research status, he developed a theoretical and methodological alternative to the French philological dominance, while building a small applied department running PR contracts. He could so maintain a dual position: on the one hand, claiming he did not want to follow the logic of the job market and, on the other, offering jobs to young graduates through his entrepreneurial endeavours. The oddity of the position exemplifies the reality of the Department.

5 The reality of the Department is essentially constituted by courses – not by research or consultancies. Professors are supposed to be in their office when not teaching; they can be at home but travelling is less easy. It is not a matter of local involvement – just a matter of physical presence at faculty meetings. International networks are not too highly valued: why would the Department need external help? Aren't we good enough? Neither is research: it is a luxury one can afford for a time, early in one's career. Dedication to teaching is the first (implicit) demand on professors. A question never asked is: what are you working on these days? In other quarters, such as the Maison des Sciences de l'Homme in Paris, everyone who plays the game knows he needs a ready answer to that constant conversational starter. No such stress in Liège.

The dominance of teaching over research (and the total lack of a graduate programme) may explain why the many curricula developed over the years never quite reflected the inner dynamics of the discipline, in terms of either research themes or research methods. Even in the bright new 1992–3 programme there are no such courses as interpersonal communication, non-verbal communication, or intercultural communication, which are so familiar to American and British curricula. Yet courses as intriguing as semantics (semasiology and onomasiology) can still be spotted. Scholars who know how awful non-verbal communication courses can be may say that semantics cannot be that bad an idea. Indeed – why not such a course? Why not resist the temptation to faddishly mimic the French, English or American communication scene? The only problem was that choices were made not with this reasoning in mind, but mostly out of ignorance. As we saw earlier, the curricula have always been built by outsiders (or by insiders who knew only too well the limits of their power to change). Most of them totally ignore the reality of communication as a discipline or as a field of research. Enough said.

Pierre Bourdieu wrote in *Homo Academicus* that power in the science faculties is based on scientific prestige; at the opposite end of the spectrum, power in the law and medicine faculties is 'formed on the accumulation of positions allowing the control of other positions and their holders' (Bourdieu 1988). The arts and social science faculties combine both kinds of academic power, from within and from without:

> Indeed, on the one hand, these faculties participate in the scientific field, and therefore in the logic of research, and the intellectual field – with the consequence that intellectual renown constitutes the only kind of capital and profit which is specifically their own; on the other hand, as institutions entrusted with the transmission of legitimate culture and invested because of this with a social function of consecration and conservation, they are places of specifically social powers, which have as much right as those of the professors of law and medicine to contribute to the most basic structures of the social order.
>
> (ibid.: 74).

The top media administrator in Belgium necessarily accumulates positions 'allowing the control of other positions and their holders; he has social power and the right to contribute to the most basic structures of the social order'. But outside academia. His power cannot be transferred into the academic field or transformed into academic power. Within the university, he has no such power 'founded principally on control of the instruments of reproduction of the professional body' (ibid.: 78). He has, moreover, very little scientific power 'founded on successful investment in the activity of research alone' (ibid.: 74), since he does not hold a doctorate, cannot list multiple publications, does not lead research teams, etc. Therefore, he has nothing; he is simply an intruder, who must be kept in the borderline position of the practitioner who comes and teaches a professional training course (although he precisely does not teach such courses – but mass communication theory courses).

The case debated on April Fool's Day 1992 illustrates a reality we tend to forget these days: the university is still a fortress, power lies within. One can only share it from the inside out; the reverse strategy (i.e. outside in) does not work. This iron rule has deep consequences for the development of a new discipline like communication: it is going to be defined by professors who do not know anything about it (at the international, scientific level, that is) but have the academic power to shape it according to their own grids, which are either naïvely pre-professional (communication is about training journalists) or scientifically absolute (communication is philology applied to non-literary works). Even the new development in Anthropology of Communication, which seems to be based more on scientific power (externally) acquired by a junior research associate turned Faculty member, can be discussed in terms of internal academic power: no real opening up can be suggested so long as the leader of the new programme still has very little authority within the University. It is not just a matter of time; it is also a matter of paying with 'one's own time', as Bourdieu put it.

> the accumulation of a specific capital of academic authority demands payment in kind, that is, with one's own time in order to control the network of institutions where . . . a capital of services rendered is gradually constituted, which is indispensable to establishment of complicities, alliances and clienteles.
>
> (ibid.: 96)

In other words, new subfields can be developed, even in Liège. The philological power base cannot entirely control the past, present and future of the Department. Yet, the accumulation of academic power which is going to be needed to ground and protect such developments will require a complete overhaul of the 'structure of the time-economy' of those in charge. It is up to them – to a large extent – to decide the fate of their Department.

This line of analysis shows that a discipline is not just a matter of ideas burgeoning here and there, as 'state of the art' reports seem to imply. It is also a matter of institutional structures, and within such structures, a matter of persons with their own trajectories, strategies and ambitions. A discipline is not the sole matter of research or graduate teaching either; it also has to do with the ways in which it is taught at the undergraduate level: conservatively or innovatively, market- or research-oriented. This is especially true of communication in French-speaking Belgium because its institutionalisation relies primarily on undergraduate teaching. Graduate work and research are still solo exercises with no solid structuration. What is taught today, and how it is taught, is going to be highly consequential for the future of the discipline, especially as far as the choice between 'skills and schemes' is concerned. Communication education may become the bed of either. The responsibility is ours.

POST SCRIPTUM

The top media administrator was finally voted in at the Faculty meeting of May 1992 – with very little opposition. Once arguments were expressed, nomination apparently turned out to be a technicality. Nobody wanted to battle again. But just wait for the next fight.

The rules of the game, however, may radically change in the next few years because of the recent dramatic increases in student population. Although the voice of the student representative was not heard at the Faculty's April Fool's Day meeting (as is most often the case in such 'high powered' gatherings), the students may soon become the next key institutional actors in the future of the Department. Two reasons may be suggested. One is very straightforward: the weight of massive figures. When the Department was only a two-year programme, there were at most 150 students around. Now that the Department offers a full four-year curriculum, more than 700 students can be expected – the size of the entire Faculty of Psychology.

For years the Department was seen as a small, immature, uncertain structure, which needed little money, few staff and little space. A strict application of a rule of proportion (so many students, so many professors, so many books, etc.) would have boosted the Department's means. But the other department chairs used the weakness of the 'young section' to maintain their own rules. For example, the library of the Department of Classics continued to receive a yearly grant just as thick as in the old days, although there were barely a few students left. New professors were regularly elected in Romance Philology, in spite of sharp decreases in the student population. Decision-makers acted through a constant denegration of the reality of the Department of Communication, as if it was transitional. Only fundamental disciplines like Latin or History were going to stay. Communication was seen as a fad, soon to disappear.

The problem is that the fad is now twenty years old and growing at a spectacular rate. It is no longer possible to deny the reality of the Department. Although a rule of proportion is still totally unthinkable (in such a case, the Department would get almost half the budget of the Faculty of Philosophy and Letters), requests for new means cannot be rejected so easily. The ratio is now a professor for a hundred students; in other departments (e.g.

sociology), the ratio is about a professor for two students. This proportion appears so unreal that changes seem to be inevitable.

The second reason for giving students a key role in the development of the Department only crystallised very recently: the weight of massive figures coupled with the 'strength of weak ties' (to recycle Granovetter's beautiful oxymoron). When students numbered only twenty or thirty, protests usually died very quickly. Every other year, there were rashes of irritation about the very poor organisation of the Department (courses cancelled without notice, ill-functioning equipment, library closed most of the time, etc.). But no structural changes were ever caused by such moves: the Faculty and the administration only had to wait for the next generation of students (the former generation would leave the university frustrated – but nobody ever considered the long-term effects of bitter alumni). In spring 1992, however, one student blow struck higher and deeper into the structures of the University. Students wrote a petition listing the very many problems plaguing the University in general and the Department in particular. The arguments were clearly and calmly written. It was not a foolish act by a few temperamental students. The petition circulated widely within the Department, reached the Board of Administration and ended up in the local media. It was not a 'scandal' – but the tremor was deep enough to help the Dean of the Faculty of Philosophy and Letters secure new financial means for upgrading a big auditorium and buying new cinema equipment (two 35 mm projectors). Such substantial upheavals usually require several attempts and several years of internal lobbying. The Dean got it all in a few weeks. This is all the more surprising in view of the fact that students did not demonstrate publicly (strikes, sit-ins, press conferences – the usual media-oriented display of collective, civil wrath). They did not have a clearly defined leadership, and their action was very short (two or three weeks in March 1992). Yet it was apparently sufficient to get the administration into gear.[4]

It is not certain that Communication students themselves have a clear realisation of their power. Rather, they believe they are totally powerless, neglected by the Faculty and rejected by the administration (except by a motherly secretary they rely on as the source of open and hidden information). After a Department meeting or two, the student representatives are usually disgruntled. Yet, that vision may change in the future. Not that there will be a repeat of May '68. Rather, in a fashion similar to Greens, who progressively learned the rules of the political game and became excellent in quietly subverting it, Communication students may emerge as well versed at flexing their muscles to get what they feel they need. In that respect, they may one day push for a more clearly defined professional relevance to their curriculum. Just wait until they get the media administrator elected as Dean of the Faculty of Philosophy and Letters.

NOTES

1 Two pieces of work proved to be very useful: a *mémoire* by Jacqueline Viatour (1988–9), who attempted to define the social profile of the Communication student, and a memo by Maurice Capitaine (1992), a former student who is also a professional librarian, and who archived documents on the history of the Department for the twentieth anniversary celebration in 1992. The following sketch is based on their work, as well as on a compilation of old course structures kindly prepared for me by Anne Jacquemin, the current secretary of the Department.
2 Cultural animation is virtually untranslatable. *L'animation culturelle* is a French (and then Belgian) concept of feeding underprivileged social groups with cultural products and activities. State-financed 'houses of culture' were installed throughout the land to that effect.
3 The hostility was sometimes very explicit. When I sent my *Nouvelle Communication* to Robert Escarpit, who then (1981) still dominated the French scene, he returned the copy with a scribbling engraved into the lamination of the cover: 'Le vieux bla-bla-bla amerloque.' Escarpit had the 'delicacy' not to return it to me directly but via my doctoral adviser, who was still one of his protégés at the time. . . .
4 A third reason can only be alluded to: parents. When the pool of students is larger, the chances of powerful parents acting behind the scene are greater. Presently, the son of the vice-Prime Minister and the daughter of the former Minister of Education are (quiet) members of the class of '94.

REFERENCES

Bourdieu, P. (1988) *Homo Academicus*, trans. Peter Collier, Cambridge: Polity Press (French original, 1984).
Capitaine, M. (1992) *Evolution de la section depuis sa création: quelques repères chronologiques*, typed note, University of Liège.
Viatour, J. (1988–9) *Origine et devenir de l'étudiant en communication*, *mémoire* in 'Arts et Sciences de la Communication', University of Liège.

Chapter 9

Communication and media studies in Sweden

Jan Ove Eriksson

Considering the ongoing changes in the media system as well as in higher education in Sweden, it is extremely difficult to provide a clear and unambiguous picture. This chapter must therefore be seen as a personal reflection on the situation. Before giving a picture of the Swedish educational system in general and education within communication sciences in particular, I will give a brief introduction to the Swedish media system and its transition since the late 1970s.

HISTORICAL BACKGROUND

The Swedish media in change

Before 1991, there was neither private broadcasting nor advertising on radio or on terrestrial television in Sweden. Although satellite channels had introduced commercial and private sector television into cabled households by the end of the 1980s, the general picture had changed little over the last decade. Some even regarded Sweden in the late 1980s as a kind of media museum trying to preserve the media system of the 1960s for the future (see Weibull and Anshelm 1992 upon which the following overview is based). Today, however, the picture of Sweden as a country of media stability would be totally misleading. I shall now try to analyse what has happened since the late 1970s.

Traditionally, newspapers play an important role on the Swedish media scene. Newspaper circulation per head of population is one of the highest in the world. Four out of five Swedes are daily readers of a morning paper, and one out of three reads an evening tabloid regularly. Newspapers are mainly local or regional – only two tabloid newspapers can be regarded as national – and are traditionally affiliated to different political parties.

As in most European countries, radio and television were introduced by a public service company. In 1955 TV was organised as a part of what was then renamed the Swedish Broadcasting Corporation. In 1969, a second television channel was started. In the late 1970s broadcasting outside this company was allowed, and voluntary organisations were permitted to establish community radio in 1978. In these new radio stations, as in the public service ones, advertising was strictly banned. At about the same time, local and regional radio was introduced inside the public service company. Swedish national television did not change very much in the 1980s. The main 'innovation' within this area was the introduction of Swedish-owned, commercial TV channels broadcasting via satellite. Since cable TV has expanded rather rapidly since 1985, satellite TV today reaches about half of the Swedish TV households.

The most expansive medium of the 1980s was radio. Radio production has increased inside as well as outside the public service sector. (In terms of hours, the volume of radio production was five times higher in 1990 than it was in 1980.) The main area of expansion has been in community radio.

Communication and media as academic and educational subjects

My starting point is that studies of communication and the media benefit from a multi-disciplinary (or interdisciplinary) approach. The various disciplines of the social sciences and humanities, for example social psychology, sociology, linguistics, semiotics, political science, are seen as helpful to an understanding of media and communication. The social sciences, on the one hand, and humanities, on the other, are not so wide apart as the administrative division of Swedish universities into different faculties seems to indicate.

In the 1960s media and communication as independent subjects of study were a relatively unexplored field. Of the Nordic countries it was virtually only in Finland that any real research was being carried out.

Since then the field may be said to have developed along the following lines:

1 A substantial expansion of academic education and research in media and communication in all the Nordic countries (partly as a result of the expansion of the media system).

2 An institutionalisation of the research field through the establishment of a number of research institutions.

Modern communication science covers a very broad field. Information, communication and mass media issues have been studied from many different angles and within a whole range of disciplines. In Swedish mass communication research one of the major issues of debate has long been whether the subject should primarily be seen as an arts subject or as a social science. A recurrent topic in this context is the extent to which the subject should be considered as a research field or as a separate academic discipline. Advocates of the former view maintain that media and communication issues should be studied by scientists and scholars with various backgrounds. Advocates of the latter view, on the other hand, claim that there is a theoretical nucleus which would justify regarding the subject as a separate discipline. Many of those working in the field today, including myself, hold that there is no simple answer to this problem. There are good reasons both for studying the field from the perspective of a whole range of academic disciplines and for pursuing the task of formulating the disciplinary nucleus of the subject.

There is in Sweden, I would venture to say, general agreement on the following delimitation of the object of study. Mass communication refers to communication processes that are:

1 *mediated*, i.e. involving some form of technical production of meaning-conveying material;

2 *organised*, i.e. involving some type of formal organisation;

3 *public*, i.e in principle accessible to all the members of some social system.

In other words mass communication cannot claim to cover all communication. The communication processes delimited here are primarily connected with the traditional media (newspapers, radio and television) but the subject also includes all kinds of technical media which are organized for communication in all types of public settings (from companies and organizations to national and global communities). This delimitation, however, does not mean that communication in the sense of 'face-to-face' interplay and interaction between people, verbal communication, communication by means of dress, gestures, etc., is excluded from courses which in various educational contexts are intended to provide knowledge about 'communication'. On the contrary, special 'micro-communication courses' are given.

I would further venture to say that there is also general agreement on the central issues to be addressed. Using McQuail (1987) as a point of departure, we may say that research on the media has come to concentrate on three different aspects: the media as a social institution, as an organisation and as an offering. There are two ways of approaching the media as a social phenomenon: first, by examining how the media relate to other types of institutions in society, for example political and economic – the conditions under which the mass media operate in society; and, second, by examining the role the media play in relation to the 'public', that is, the role of the mass media in society.

Especially within sociology, the discipline I represent, concepts/approaches which emerged and were developed to answer the initial needs of scientific development are now changing. Concepts such as class and structure, developed within a sociology trying to understand the industrial and work society, no longer grasp society we now label post-industrial, postmodern or information technological. When social interaction and social integration in a society become more and more dependent on consumption, including the consumption of signs, we need to complement the old approaches and the old concepts of sociology with other concepts and methods. This means that we can now see much broader research perspectives in operation, widening the field of phenomena to be studied. Studies of the products of popular culture and communication are knocking at the doors of many different university departments and are gradually being let in.

The roots of communication science in Sweden are to be found in the arts. One of the first to be interested in the study of the modern daily press was a man who became Professor of Literature in Gothenburg in 1901. Early press research generally adopted an historical perspective with the aim of elucidating the growth and contents of the media. However, in the 1950s, a number of social science disciplines addressed the issue of the role of the mass media in society and their effect on the population. For methodological reasons, the media were seen as part of a communication process. Sociologists, political scientists and economists were pioneers in Swedish mass media research within the social sciences. During the 1970s collaboration between media scientists with different academic backgrounds intensified, with the result that mass communication has now developed and become established as an independent educational and research field. The subject has undergone specialisation with the establishment of specific research and teaching institutions for information and/or mass media studies. At the same time, it has retained its institutional multiplicity. There are, in fact, still a large number of 'bearers' of the subject spread over various, more traditional university disciplines (e.g. sociology, political science). A national survey of research in 1989 reported 97 major projects and 29 doctoral theses distributed between more than 40 different research institutions.

UNDERGRADUATE COURSES IN COMMUNICATION

The higher education system in Sweden is fundamentally a public system. There is only, currently, one private unit: the Stockholm School of Commerce. The higher education system consists of 35 universities and colleges. The number of students has increased only marginally since 1970, but the total number of employees has been increasing considerably as a result of the state higher education policy, which has on the whole been very favourable towards academia. Some conclusions can be drawn (Lane 1991). A major process of decentralisation has been undertaken, involving a break with the dominant mode of centralised decision-making in the Swedish higher educational system. The tasks of the central authority, the National Board of Universities and Colleges (NBUC), have been reoriented towards evaluation and monitoring. Regional co-ordination boards have been abolished, placing the main responsibility for planning within the local institutions themselves. Quality has replaced equality as the guiding principle in higher education.

Complete BA programmes in communication science are offered at the Universities of Karlstad, Örebro, Växjö, Jönköping and Sundsvall. Separate single-subject courses in the field are offered by the universities in Umeå, Gothenburg, Stockholm, Uppsala and Lund. Postgraduate studies are also available at these universities and most research is conducted there.

Studies in communication/information are among the most

popular undergraduate programmes in terms of the number of applications in the University of Karlstad and Sweden as a whole. For example, the total number of applications in Karlstad for the academic year 1991–2 was about 1,200. The number of available places is only 24 at present. Seen over the period from 1977 to 1992, the main goals of the programme may be said to have shifted from 'being able to produce' (the 1970s) via 'being able to produce/communicate' (the 1980s) to 'being able to communicate' (the 1990s) after having completed the course. This 'local change' in programme character is a reflection of a general change in programmes/courses throughout Sweden. In other words, there has been a development towards a more theoretical profile.

At the University of Karlstad a considerable amount of time has been spent in recent years on developing the Communication Studies programme, with the overriding aim, naturally, of being able to offer a course of the highest possible quality. High quality in education is, of course, not an unambiguous term. For us, the measure of quality is to provide knowledge which will meet future needs rather than simply educate people for the present. Another measure of good quality might be to give students the necessary skills to analyse, evaluate and assess the new problems they will meet in their future career.

A basic condition for good quality is the knowledge and competence of the academic staff. Within such a broad field as 'media and communication' we have found it natural to engage academic staff from several disciplines. In Karlstad, the theoretical tradition lies in the social sciences in general and in sociology in particular. It is also vital for staff to have time for their own research and development. How far the subject will be able to live up to these quality demands in the future depends, we believe, on how closely undergraduate studies can be linked to research.

For this reason we believe that it is of considerable urgency to devote more time to research and development projects than has been the case up until now. We hope that we will be able to formalize the collaboration, in both teaching and research, with the section for Mass Communication at Gothenburg University which we have already initiated.

We also believe that it is important to subject examination forms to continual scrutiny and to attempt to 'implant' the attitude that examinations should be seen not as a control mechanism but rather as an integral part of a learning process. Thus, in Karlstad, we have a system whereby examinations generally take place five weeks after the start of a particular section of a course. (We are, at present, considering whether we should change this and introduce a system where students are examined on longer sections of a course, perhaps by external examiners.)

In order to measure the quality of the programme, continuous course evaluations are conducted with the students. Each section of a course normally concludes with such an evaluation, in which the students are given an opportunity to evaluate the course, and the lecturer, either separately or against the background of the students' evaluation, makes his own evaluation. Since these evaluations tend to be too related to short sub-courses, we have also started an evaluation project for the whole programme, the aim being to enable students to give their view of the programme on a number of occasions during their studies and thus provide us with feedback.

In recent years the internationalisation of Swedish higher education has been given high priority; this is true of the University of Karlstad in general and the programme in Communication Studies in particular. (One consequence is this chapter.) We have determined guidelines for the internationalisation of the programme, which involve staff and student exchanges with foreign universities, study visits to other countries, more course books in languages other than Swedish and the introduction of more international issues into the content of our courses.

When it comes to granting recognition for studies abroad, we are of the opinion that it is important to adopt a liberal attitude and allow the students to make their own selection of courses.

The courses which we will be able to offer incoming students will include both regular courses and courses which are tailor-made to meet the needs of these students (this also involves the issue of the language of tuition).

The University of Karlstad is a fairly young university. It was founded in 1977 through the amalgamation of Karlstad University College (founded in 1967 in affiliation with Gothenburg University) and Karlstad Teacher Training College (founded in 1843). At present it has 7,000 students and 450 staff.

The University offers a wide range of programmes and courses in technology and engineering, economics and the social sciences, the arts and teaching training. All teaching and research is housed in one building with good opportunities for informal working methods, inter-disciplinary co-operation, integration, flexibility and, of special interest to me, more direct lines of communication. Research at the University is mainly organized in ten independent multi-disciplinary units. Attached to the University is a science park, whose purpose is to provide a meeting place where the University and commerce and industry in the region can exchange knowledge and experience. Today the university offers 25 study programmes and separate single-subject courses in approximately 40 different subjects.

One such subject is communication science, which, since 1977, has been taught in the form of a BA in Communication Studies and some single-subject courses on a part-time basis.

The aim of our programme in Communication Studies is to provide the student with basic knowledge and skills in the field, and to further independent critical thinking on communication. In this context the student learns to identify, analyse and solve communication problems in both the public and private sectors of Swedish working life and in organizations. A broad social science and humanistic perspective is adopted, which entails studying communication in its political, economic, social and cultural context. The role of language is stressed and the student receives training in visual, oral and writing skills.

The programme requires three years' (six terms) full-time study. (The length of courses and programmes in Swedish universities is indicated by a points system where 40 points represents one academic year's full-time study). During the fifth term the student may choose any option he or she wishes, including a period of study abroad. The courses in the other five terms are, at this moment, mandatory.

The content is designed to develop the student's ability to understand the demands placed on the professional communicator. Further, it provides up-to-date information on research in the field. During his or her studies the student acquires:

- insight into groups, organisations and society as systems and the individual's communicative role in them;
- knowledge of the structure of Swedish and international media, of their function and of the conditions under which they operate, for instance the consequences of developments in media technology;

- knowledge of basic scientific theories and perspectives relevant to communication;
- knowledge of the legal framework for information and communication;
- awareness of the role of language as a medium of communication;
- oral and writing skills and basic skills in working with various media;
- knowledge of scientific methods and their application to information and communication; basic skills in the specific methods in the field;
- insight into ethical issues having bearing on the profession.

The following courses are studied:

Term 1: *The Individual in a Social and Cultural Context.* 20 points
The course includes a basic study of language, information and communication and considers the role of the professional communicator and communication in a social context. Further topics include basic linguistic theory, humans as cultural beings and humans and their environment in sociological, socio-psychological and political perspective.

Term 2: *Means and Methods of Information Production.* 20 points
The course considers the various means and methods of producing information. After completing the course, the student should have both the theoretical knowledge and skills needed for the production of printed material, for desk-top publishing, for radio and TV/video work. Special emphasis is placed on language.

Term 3: *Communication Science (basic course).* 20 points
The course begins with basic communication theory, including language and the socio-psychological aspects of communication. It then goes on to examine more macro-oriented approaches to information and communication, for instance the structure of Swedish and international media. There is a final section where communication theory and planning are integrated. Basic research and survey methods are also included.

Term 4: *Communication Science (intermediate course)*. 20 points Further studies in communication theory; communication in organizations is studied within the framework of organizational theory. Various legal issues are considered. The course concludes with a work placement. Research and survey methods are studied in more detail.

Term 5: *Unspecified option*. 20 points

Term 6: *Communication Science (advanced course)*. 20 points This consists of a study of epistemology and scientific methods, as well as advanced communication theory, including the study of both classical and modern theories. It also includes a degree project.

THE FUTURE

Sweden's social structure has undergone considerable changes, which have also resulted in changes in the communication structure. More and more media have emerged and a major reconstruction of the media industry is in progress. (For instance, we have a new commercial television channel and the introduction of commercial radio is under discussion.) Other major changes are the result of various technological developments.

There are, of course many reasons, for Karlstad's investment in internationalisation: 'achieving an international perspective', 'gaining new cultural experiences' and 'improving language skills', just to mention a few. Internationalisation has also had consequences for the way in which higher education is organized in Sweden. The National Swedish Board of Universities and Colleges has decided to introduce a new examination system, one object being to give a clearer picture of Swedish higher education in an international context. From the autumn of 1993 the student will simply have to meet the general requirements for a Bachelor's or Master's degree in a particular field. The choice of options within the field will be largely his or her own.

At the same time, central planning documents will be abolished and each university and college will itself be responsible for the content and organisation of the courses of study it offers. An examination system of this type, it is hoped, will enable us to adapt to European examination praxis and thus improve our competitiveness in the international community. Since this change will 'soften' the present emphasis in the Swedish university system on fairly rigid programmes, individual choice will play a more crucial role. The current requirement that university education should have 'a vocational' bias will thus be toned down, with the result, we hope, that more students will eventually go on to postgraduate studies.

We believe that, in the future, it will be essential to see higher education and research as basically international in nature. The university symbolizes the lack of frontiers in several respects: it needs international contacts and even perhaps international quality control. Some of the essential features of activities of this type are:

- participation in international research and educational programmes of the ERASMUS type. Within these programmes it will be possible either to find common profiles and agree on the direction of the course, or simply to plan completely different profiles. Increased mobility of the labour market presupposes some form of co-operation of this type;
- promotion of international databases;
- an attempt to utilise new technical aids in distance teaching. Efforts to gain support for the development of technical aids, communication techniques which can be used independently of national frontiers, language, etc. (cf. COMETT).

If higher education should in general become more international, the need is particularly acute for the study of communication.

REFERENCES

Eskola, K. (1991) *Communication, Articulation and Representation*, Gothenburg: Nordicom-Information.
Lane, J. E. (1991) 'Sweden in the aftermath of educational reform', in B. Neave and F. van Vught (eds) *Prometheus Bound*, Oxford: Pergamon Press.
McQuail, D. (1987) *Masscommunication Theory: An Introduction*, London: Sage.
Weibull, L. and Anshelm, M. (1992) *Signs of Change: Swedish Media in Transition*, Gothenburg: Nordicom-Information.

Chapter 10

Communication science and broadcasting in the Netherlands

Ard Heuvelman

This chapter will deal with the curricula for communication science at universities in the Netherlands and the way in which these curricula prepare students for problems in public broadcasting. I wish to emphasise that there is a great need for communication managers, in general but particularly in broadcasting: these are people who combine knowledge and skills in communication (theories) with knowledge and skills in management (theories). In the Netherlands this need is particularly urgent because of the changing situation in public broadcasting. I will show how the University of Twente tries to fill this existing gap in communications education with a new curriculum.

COMMUNICATION EDUCATION IN THE NETHERLANDS

Communication science

At most of the universities in Holland's neighbour countries, Germany and Belgium, communication science has been a substantive discipline for many years now, attracting large numbers of students. In the Netherlands we are only at the beginning of such a development, since communication science was not officially acknowledged until 1982, in the Law of Scientific Education.

At this moment there are two universities in the Netherlands preparing students for a Master's degree in Communication Science. They both have a three-year curriculum (5,040 hours) and students who have finished a first year in one of the social sciences are allowed on to the programme. One is at the Catholic University of Nijmegen, in the Faculty of Social Sciences. The other one is at the University of Amsterdam, in the Faculty of Political and Social Cultural Sciences. The two curricula are primarily directed towards the study of mass communications. They both are social scientific studies; the study of media technology is secondary. Students are not trained to become professional communicators. In the Netherlands professional skills in, for instance, journalism, graphic design, film-making, etc., are taught at schools of higher vocational education and academies of art, and not at the universities.

The University of Amsterdam has the following programme:

Base Level

1 Introduction to Theories and Models of Communication;
2 Theory and Research on the Communication Processes;
3 Content of Messages and Effects of Messages.

Middle Level

1 Communication Research (methods and techniques);
2 Media Systems and Organisation (historic development and actual situation);
3 Audience Research (fundamental aspects of information processing and persuasion, and functions, processes, and effects of mass communication);
4 Information, Administration and Business (information-supply for business, in the context of organizations and new technologies).

Specialist Level

1 Media Organization and Policy;
2 History of Communication;
3 Audience Research;
4 Cultural Media Studies;
5 Information Science

The programme at the University of Nijmegen is as follows:

General Courses

1 Introduction to Communication Science;
2 Overview of Media;
3 Research Methods;

4 Statistics.

Extension Courses

1 Media Consumption;
2 Media Policy;
3 Theories of Communication Science;
4 Information and Public Relations;
5 Advertising and Propaganda;
6 Audiovisual Communication;
7 Content Analysis;
8 Social and Political Philosophy;
9 Skills.

Specialist Courses

1 Media and Society;
2 Mass Communications and Culture;
3 Small-Scale Communication;
4 Functional Communication Science.

Other disciplines

Besides the curricula of Communication Science in Amsterdam and Nijmegen, there are a number of other disciplines which pay attention to communication in their courses. Traditionally this has been the case in several departments of (social) psychology in the Netherlands. Although psychology is primarily a research-oriented discipline, one can see a growing interest in psychological aspects of communication and an orientation towards professions of communication. A similar development can be observed in departments of (applied) linguistics, with an emphasis on skills in written communication. There are also a number of specializations in other disciplines where optional courses in Communication are offered, because distribution of information plays an important part, for instance, in health education or agricultural science.

Since September 1990 the State University of Utrecht has offered courses in Mass Communication and Public Relations. Students from various disciplines can obtain a special certificate in Communication.

What all these courses in the Netherlands – Communication Science and others – have in common, is that they attract large numbers of students. Communications education is very popular in Holland.

THE CHANGING SITUATION IN BROADCASTING

Cultural changes

Public broadcasting in the Netherlands started in 1924 on radio. Licences were given to broadcasting companies of any religious or political persuasion, Roman Catholic, Protestant or socialist. They all made their programmes for a fixed and faithful audience: only Catholics listened to programmes of the Catholic broadcasting company, only socialists to those of the socialist broadcasting company, etc.

After the Second World War, this situation gradually changed. With the rise of television people began to watch programmes, instead of channels, with a specific affiliation. Other broadcasters, without roots in any ideological movement, were allowed into the organisation of public broadcasting.

Still, the basic structure remains unchanged. Everybody in Holland possessing a TV set has to pay a compulsory licence fee of 160 guilders. Everybody from the age of 16 can become a member of one or more broadcasting companies or associations. The amount of broadcasting time each of those (eight) companies has depends entirely on the number of members they have. The companies are independent, that is to say, free from government interference, but are required to provide a programme package which includes cultural and educational programming as well as information and entertainment. The Netherlands Broadcasting Corporation (NOS) has an 'umbrella function'. The NOS has no members from the public, in fact its members are the other broadcasting organisations themselves. It provides a number of services and facilities for the other organisations.

Expansion of cable networks

Holland has become a country with a very dense cable network, which connects about 85 per cent of the population. In most areas more than twenty different channels can be received: this means a widespread reception of not only the three Dutch public channels, but also those of Belgium, Great Britain, Germany, a few

French, one or two Italian, and a number of commercial stations, like RTL4, RTL+, CNN, MTV, Super Channel, Eurosport.

Commercialisation of broadcasting

The public broadcasting associations are financed by membership fees and by the revenues from advertising blocks on the public channels. Both sources of financing are under pressure nowadays. Membership of a broadcasting company is connected with subscription to a TV-guide. Every company puts out one or even two TV-guides at extremely low prices to attract as many members as possible. In fact, many people do not really support the ideology of their broadcasting association but are members because of the magazine. The eight companies are the only organisations in Holland allowed to publish advance programme details, so they meet no competition on this market. However, it is very questionable whether this national regulation can hold out against international law.

International satellites have bypassed national regulations protecting public broadcasting services. Since the beginning of 1990 a commercial Dutch network, RTL4, based in Luxembourg has been in operation. It is only available on cable, but has been a great success in terms of rating figures. This success has precipitated a decline in commercials on the public channels and, consequently, a loss of income.

Competition for the audience

The success of a channel in terms of rating figures depends more and more on good channel management. Popularity of programmes depends on the competition they meet on other channels at the same time. Since the advent of RTL4, good channel management has suddenly become a necessity in Dutch public broadcasting. The average Dutch viewer watches about two hours of TV per day. Despite the expansion of the number of channels on the cable, this viewing time has been fairly stable over the years. Moreover, viewing time is spent almost entirely watching Dutch programmes – those of the three public channels and RTL4.

All this means that competition on Dutch television is very strong, even between the public associations, because although they are non-commercial, they are in fact competitors with each other since they depend on the membership of the audience. On the other hand, the public associations are forced to co-operate with each other in order to compete with the commercial channel RTL4.

This strong competition demands a more market-oriented approach to broadcasting and also highly qualified people to manage these processes; qualified in terms of communication theories and strategies, research-oriented, with knowledge of the economics of broadcasting and of laws and regulations, and with management skills.

PROBLEMS OF MANAGEMENT IN BROADCASTING

Who decides what in Dutch broadcasting?

One might think that members of the broadcasting associations in the Netherlands have a great say in the affairs and the programming of their companies, in other words that the audience has a great influence. However, with one exception (VPRO), this is not the case. The companies are organisations with a specific 'culture'. Each company used to be run by a chairman recruited from its own ideological grouping, with heads of departments for radio and television recruited from its own programme-makers and producers.

The changing situation in public broadcasting made transformations of most of the company cultures necessary. Some companies are now run by ex-politicians who know their way in government circles in the Hague, while radio and television departments are run by business managers. In many companies interim managers were appointed 'to muck out the stables'; these were often managers with a background in economy and business, and not in communication, let alone broadcasting. People in key positions with great experience in programme-making and broadcasting have almost become extinct.

This process has caused some serious problems in many broadcasting companies.

Management and programme-makers

Several problems have arisen between management and programme-makers. By management I mean the people responsible for managing and policy-making in the companies and by programme-makers the people involved in the production of the programmes for radio and television. Programme-makers have several complaints about their company staff:

• The staff only have eyes for rating figures; there is no time for programme development – a programme must 'score' immediately.
• The new management have no ideas about programme development and know nothing of actual programme-making, yet they decide on these matters.
• Radio programmes are neglected; television is the only thing that counts.
• Good channel management is lacking.

The new management have a business-like attitude. However, it is one thing to sell soap, but quite another to 'sell' soap operas.

Management and researchers

With the changing situation in broadcasting more time and money are spent on research. The management of the companies want to play safe in their decisions on programmes, programming, magazines and policy regarding membership. More and more programmes are pre-tested before broadcasting, but there is also a lot of evaluation research on programmes, on strategies to obtain and to keep new members, and research on the public image of the companies.

All this demands communications research. However, most of the managers in broadcasting are clearly unfamiliar with this kind of research and this unfamiliarity produces problems with both the formulation of good research questions and the implementation of research outcomes.

In this respect the new management are willing, but not able.

THE NEED FOR COMMUNICATION MANAGERS

The problems in Dutch public broadcasting are similar to the problems in other organisations where communication management is important. In a way they are similar to problems in business or administration in general. That is why communication advice bureaux are a 'booming' business in the Netherlands. When there are communication problems in an organisation, it engages such a bureau. Most organisations in the Netherlands are not able to solve their own communication problems because of a lack of in-house communication management. This holds true also for the broadcasting organizations in the Netherlands.

Combining qualities

Public broadcasting companies in the Netherlands need professional managers with knowledge of communication theories and processes; with knowledge of rules and regulations, of communication strategies, of communication research, knowledge about the world of broadcasting in general – people who combine knowledge and skills in communication (theories) with knowledge and skills in management (theories).

Communications education in the Netherlands does not supply such people: in the current curricula little attention is paid to policy-making and administration, but no attention at all is paid to management theories and skills. That is the main reason why broadcasting companies in the Netherlands have little or no room for communication students on key positions in their organisations. No one starts, of course, as a manager in an organisation, but knowledge and skills do help to accelerate the process of becoming one. Communication students have, up till now, been almost exclusively appointed to research jobs in broadcasting.

A proposal

The University of Twente has received approval for the introduction of a new curriculum in 1993. The programme is called 'Applied Communication Science'. It lasts for four years (6,720 hours), leads to a Master's degree, and is characterised by five essential elements:

- communication theories from various relevant disciplines;
- research methods;
- management and policy;
- design of communication systems and communication policy;
- communication techniques.

The programme will be an interdisciplinary enterprise: four different faculties will be involved:

- the Faculty of Philosophy and Social sciences (Departments of Psychology and Applied Linguistics);
- the Faculty of Instructional Science (Departments of Instruction Technology and Instrumentation Technology);
- the Faculty of Public Administration and Public Policy (Department of Political Science);
- the Faculty of Business Administration (Department of Social Management).

The general part of the programme takes 3,720 hours and consists of six main areas:

1 Communication Theories;
2 Research Methods and Techniques;
3 Design of Communication Systems;
4 Communication Techniques;
5 Public and Business Administration;
6 Supporting Courses (Philosophy and English).

The specialist or differential part of the programme takes 3,000 hours. At this stage the students have to choose two of the following specializations:

1 Information Supply Systems;
2 Persuasion and Social Psychology;
3 Media Techniques and Production;
4 Applied Linguistics;
5 Public Administration;
6 Business Administration.

This curriculum has been shown to several leading communication experts in the Netherlands for evaluation and comments. The experts came from business companies, public policy, advertising bureaux, communication advice bureaux and broadcasting. The evaluations were quite positive. The experts think that this curriculum will train students to become communication managers in the various parts of the 'field' of communication – people who are now lacking in organisations, because the existing curricula do not supply them.

In public broadcasting, people trained both in media techniques and production and, for instance, business administration would be unique.

APPENDIX: THE THREE PUBLIC TV CHANNELS IN THE NETHERLANDS, OCTOBER 1992

N1
AVRO: Liberal but decent
KRO: Roman Catholic
NCRV: Protestant
(NOS: Youth, news, sports)

N2
Veronica: Popular youth programmes
TROS: Popular family programmes
EO: Reformed
(Teleac: Educational programmes)
(NOS: News, sports)

N3
VARA: Social Democrats
VPRO: Anarcho-Liberals
NOS: Public interest, news, sports

Chapter 11

Communication knowledge, communication beliefs
Their educational and social implications

Axel Gryspeerdt

The debate on communication education and research cannot be conducted without consideration of those belief systems affecting the way communication is thought about. For this reason, it is important that those involved in communication are aware of their beliefs as well as of the various communication discourses in circulation. These discourses have developed profoundly in recent years, becoming increasingly numerous and diverse; in less than twenty years, the number of those considered either by themselves or by others to be legitimate commentators on communication has become staggering. Communication libraries have been established and specialised bookshops opened to house the growing range of publications on the subject.

We are today far from the situation of the 1960s and 1970s, during which period the dominant communication discourses were relatively homogeneous and straightforward. The places in which these discourses were discussed and circulated were limited, and students and researchers knew which sources to consult and the credit which they should be given. Important sources considered relevant to communication[1] were few, and fairly concise. They were distinguished by an institutionalised, rule-governed approach and an organisational ('How should the media be structured and organised?') and empirical ('How can effects be measured?') orientation. They were mainly dedicated to information systems (known as 'media', or more usually 'mass media'), and to the machinery of persuasion.

The only divergent voice at this time was that of Marshall McLuhan, almost a demi-god of the epoque. McLuhan was considered by some to be the first 'writer' on communication. He was diverse in many ways, his work made up simultaneously of knowledge and myth, considered ideas and intuitive beliefs, observation methods and 'penetration methodology', originality and literary reference. In drawing on the experience of the senses, on literature and art as well as the world of science, McLuhan wonderfully illustrated the process by which fiction could be felt in 'scientific works'. His 'guru' quality, his comprehensiveness (everything to do with communication and nothing but communication; advertised, televised, even telephonic and mechanical) and the generation of critical trends around him and his work (with him, communication became the object of public debate) earned him an audience of more than just specialists, and a renown amongst an intellectual class eager to know more. Under these circumstances, we should not be surprised by McLuhan's influence (direct or indirect, positive or negative) on subsequent writing and teaching. Nor should we be surprised by the misrepresentations to which his work was subjected, and the resultant 'errors' in the dissemination of his ideas. Even today, collective consciousness remembers his 'Massage and Message' work (1967) as 'The Medium is the Message', a situation reminiscent of an absurd scene from a 'Pink Panther' film in which Inspector Clouseau and the person he is speaking to fail to understand each other; one speaks massage while the other speaks message.

THE MULTIPLICATION OF 'AUTHORITATIVE' COMMUNICATION DISCOURSES

In the early to mid-1980s, both this dominant discourse and these 'McLuhanian' developments gave way to a multiple, profuse discourse. Europeans entered the debate alongside American commentators (whose standing now seemed to diminish – perhaps because the debate had until then been conducted mainly in English?), and a variety of other authors asserted the right to comment on communication. The simultaneous development of belief in a 'communication society' during this period can hardly be seen as pure coincidence; legitimate communication discourses were growing and diversifying at the same time that the expression 'communication society' was enjoying an ever greater popularity.

People from different horizons, those who spoke, wrote and published on communication, were now becoming more numerous, and beginning to replace (or, more precisely, supplement) those groups previously seen as the legitimate commentators.

In the 1960s and 1970s, the right to comment on communication was assumed only by certain people, of whom three main groups can be distinguished: owners of the media; broadcast or newspaper journalists; researchers and teachers. These groups had given the impression that they were the sole holders of the right to speak on communication, but during the 1980s a wide variety of people joined the throng: organisational advisers; consultants; educationalists; politicians; the heads of businesses and organisations.

For example, bosses became 'legitimate' commentators on communication. It even became acceptable, notably in France and Belgium, for trendy, 'media-wise' bosses to promote their communication as a model for others. The prototypes of these 'communicating their own communication' bosses were widely popularised, regardless of their area of activity or the size of their businesses (examples include Bernard Tapie, Jacques Seguela, Francis Bouygues, Claude Bebear, Philippe Bodson). Indeed, the organisation or firm itself, as an entity, has been considered since the 1980s[2] to be a 'communicating being' or communicative interface; the organisation appears to have secured its place in the chorus of communication on communication.

There are other, tangible indications that more people, of increasingly diverse qualification, have been granted (or have granted themselves) the legitimacy to comment on communication.

1 The number of books published on the subject of communication stands out as the first indication, since in recent years it has grown considerably. At present, every good academic or university bookshop has a 'communication' shelf, although booksellers are invariably confused by the varying types and complexity of the works to be found there (personal accounts, practical manuals, scientific books, guides to good communication, etc.). In major capitals, there are even specialised communication bookshops (Techné in Paris is a good example), with wide-ranging collections of communication books and reports.

2 Communication practitioners more and more frequently participate in communication colloquia or study days, whether passively (through giving assistance) or even actively. They contribute to the refinement of communication discourses in lobbying, information and news, and lend experience and expertise, whatever the field.

3 There now exist radio and television programmes enabling
  people representing vastly different areas of society to comment
  on communication issues. Examples of these phenomena (albeit
  limited to Belgium) are the '*micro-media*' or '*fait divers*' radio
  broadcasts, accessible to a wide variety of commentators.

A VAST BODY OF PRACTICAL AND THEORETICAL COMMUNICATION KNOWLEDGE

One of the significant effects of this participation and debate is that
people of widely different perspectives and practical experience
(unionists, jurors, financial experts, politicians, publishers, members of the clergy, teachers, etc.) are brought together within the
same 'space': 'media space', the editorial space of the bookshop
shelf, the physical space of the colloquium with the accompanying
social gratification that collectivity brings. These people relate to
each other both as knowledge-'seekers' and as 'contributors'
to knowledge (producers of knowledge). On the one hand, they
themselves are valorised by the questions they ask, self-
interrogation being a valued practice in a 'communication society'.
On the other hand, they disseminate communication knowledge
and beliefs, sharing them out amongst those they mingle with. In
this way a vast practical and/or theoretical knowledge or a 'model
of collective belief' in communication is constructed.[3]

There are currently so many communication beliefs in circulation that listing them all is a difficult task, and identifying the
established or verifiable 'facts' among them virtually impossible;
so many are supported by widely differing ideas and data. The
most we can do, consequently, is provide some examples of the
common-sense 'facts', although it is doubtful whether a serious
study could confirm their validity (all the more so since most of
them are postulates, rather than hypotheses proposed for
verification).

A VAST BODY OF BELIEF IN QUASI-MAGICAL EFFECTS

Among the main contemporary beliefs in communication, we can
include the following:

1 The belief that the media (and communication itself) wield great
  power. These beliefs are often articulated as communication

ideas, proverbs or phrases, and are used as if the epitome of good communication sense. It is likely that the titles of influential publications on the subject act as reminders of established communication ideas, for while the contents of these books (misread if at all, or poorly understood) are often far subtler, their more 'radical' titles (*Hidden Persuasion, How to Persuade, The Powers of Television, The Power to Inform, Persuasion and Power, Propaganda, New Political Force', How to Win an Election, Rape of the Masses by Political Propaganda*, etc.) firmly fix in collective consciousness the notion of an all-powerful media and communication.[4]

2 The belief in the importance of communication. These days, communication is seen as a solution to all sorts of problems, obstacles, crises and constraints. How many times has it been heard, in relation to the problems of a business, an organisation, a collectivity or a household, the magic formula: 'Isn't your real problem one of communication?'

3 The belief in 'constant' communication. According to this belief, even the most insignificant, the most invisible, the most discrete, the most secret, will bear some social meaning and signification. There are authors such as Pierre-Henri Jeudy in France, who now vehemently criticise this 'proverb-idea'.

4 The belief that communication can always be improved, articulated in manuals with forceful titles such as 'Communication is like Chinese, it must be learned'.

5 The belief in a communication or information society. This belief is not easy to establish, since the ambiguity and interchangeability of the two themes would confuse even the most critical and well informed.

We thus have a vast group of beliefs, undoubtedly still incomplete, which lend value to all (or at least some) of those who convey them. The sharing of these beliefs occurs all the more since the very act of divulging them reassures their speakers, and confirms their self-importance. Moreover, these beliefs not only arouse the 'community' of self-appointed communicators, they also generate meaning as 'collective perceptions', becoming as it were the ready-made ideas of every modern individual. Prominence should be given to the difficulty or the impossibility (particularly for those who do not study science) of being able to separate these beliefs from the facts which could be more properly

founded on a scientific model. To this difficulty in evaluation we
might add the fact that in a field popularised to a large extent by
media people and researchers themselves, ideas are often disseminated in an over-simplified form, or with a different meaning
altogether. We have already observed that the very famous and
controversial Marshall McLuhan gave birth to the idea (itself
hardly if at all disseminated by him) of the 'Message as Medium'.

Consequently, it is hardly surprising that, based on scraps of
practical and theoretical knowledge (the latter often 'censured' or
deformed by simplification or misunderstanding), a vast body of
belief in quasi-magical effects has been built up. Everyone feels
they are well-versed in communication debate, and the situation
is exacerbated all the more by the apparent wide-spread understanding of communication theory.

THE UNIQUE CREDIBILITY OF COMMUNICATION

At its extreme, this collective thought or social perception
increases the status of communication; it develops a form of credibility as a solution to problems and a source of power. At the
same time the status of all those involved in communication is
boosted, whether they be bosses, journalists, politicians or 'media
types' of any sort (even advertising or media organisations). That
communication enhances the status of all these groups does not,
however, preclude the fact that there are variations in the way
they are perceived; in recent years, confidence in media news
seems to have diminished while communication has retained its
credibility intact. We thus find ourselves in a paradoxical or
ambivalent situation, according to which:

- the media are doubted – the years 1990–2 demonstrated to the
  public the susceptibility of the media to error or manipulation
  (the Gulf War, events in Romania, etc.);
- journalists are simultaneously objects of admiration and suspicion – admired for their social role, for their position in
  society and the influence their prestige generates, and suspected
  due to 'proof' of their failures or possibility of error (largely
  denounced);[5]
- communication is simultaneously credible as a magic formula,
  a diagnosis or prescription ('You've got a communication
  problem') and a courageous skill;

- non-journalistic communication functions (*'dir-coms'*,[6] bosses, political or public communication consultants, advertising executives), while not being confused with journalists, are treated as communication experts.

In recent years, American and European research has, in cooperation with these corps of communicators, attempted to describe their 'professional values'; the communicators for their part have begun to 'use' the research for their own corporate and professional ends. In Europe, the research has for the most part highlighted the distrust or respect with which the different professions relate to each other (see Dagnaud 1991).

However, it can be noted that today, in their corporate battles or defence, these professional bodies do not hesitate to use scientific communication knowledge. There are currently numerous communication professionals who cite research studies, and circulate them in a popularised form.Thus, Erik Neveu and Remy Rieffel noted in their 1991 study of the effects of communication theory in France that 50 per cent of the names cited in the bibliographies of communication practitioners were those of researchers and academics (Neveu and Rieffel 1991: 33). There is a second phenomenon mentioned by Neveu and Rieffel; the construction by communication practitioners of an 'indigenous' or autonomous knowledge, a knowledge developed by these professionals based on their experience. Undoubtedly the professionals are reassured in this endeavour by societal belief in the power of communication and the legitimacy accorded them due to their posts, their prestige, their experiences, the media they cite, even the welcome they receive from the scientific community (in colloquia, courses, study days, conferences). Communication practitioners are frequently showered with diplomas, or follow supplementary, specialised communication courses.

Because of their social potency (an empirical measure of which is the impact these professionals and directors have on students, the future professionals), the knowledge imparted by practitioners tends to attract greater acclaim and credibility than that of scientific researchers. This latter group are less 'mediatised'; the knowledge they impart is more full of jargon and, by dint of a more scientific presentation or appearance, less accessible.

Despite this, as Neveu and Rieffel point out, it would be simplifying things to assume that these two groups (scientists and professionals) are in opposition. Indeed, they have much in common: they meet regularly in the same 'space' (described above), and they have dual identities (professional/teacher, professor/consultant, etc.). However, these similarities should not obscure the fact that well-founded scientific discoveries, grounded in specific discourses and practices and consequently open to debate and verification (Verhagen 1990), take an enormous amount of time to prove or disprove, whereas other more 'invented' discoveries (invented if only in the sense of their dubious scientific verification) rapidly become popularised, particularly by opinion leaders and 'mediators'. We will not return here to the errors in the explanation of McLuhan, but we will point out nevertheless that some scientific theories have taken a long time to circulate, or have yet to be widely disseminated; from agenda-setting theory to the more recent 'creative audience' theories (even the work of the very 'mediatised' Umberto Eco).

Despite their hybrid character and their collaboration with the other assorted members of the communication world, the group one would describe as 'communication opinion formers' seem none the less to be quite an ambiguous clan. Nurtured on communication theory or pseudo-theory, they seek to rub shoulders with the intellectual classes while the latter for their part tend to bestow upon them the rather ambiguous title of communication 'gurus', a phenomenon undoubtedly worthy of investigation.

THE PASSION FOR COMMUNICATION

The various facts we have highlighted, to which others could be added (for example, the rising demand from young people, increasingly considered excessive, for training in communication; the appointment of people in a communication capacity to organisations of all types, itself affecting the demand for training; the creation within the media of centres dedicated to the media themselves and to meta-communication, particularly under the rubric of 'enterprise', 'management', 'new media technology'), tend to support what we feel is a strong hypothesis. According to this, non-material investment in communication (comprising training and recruitment) has been a more significant feature of the 1980s than the creation of communication equipment and the communication infrastructure. This hypothesis is particularly plausible in a country such as Belgium, which in the 1960s and 1970s saw the development of an audiovisual infrastructure (the first teledistribution cabling, heralding a multiple choice of TV channels), a specialised, non-daily press and the instruments of internal and external organisational communication.[7]

By contrast with this situation it seems as if communication debate and discourse suddenly multiplied, simultaneously giving communication the status of social problem (or social preoccupation and problematic) and of universal solution to society's problems.

ORGANISE THE MEDIA OR ORGANISE BY USING COMMUNICATION

If the main works published in Belgium and France before the 1980s are taken as an indication, we can see with hindsight that the dominant issue of the previous two decades (expressed in books dealing with communication) was none other than the creation and development of the media. 'Concrete' questions predominated, such as 'How should television be organised?' or 'How should the press be organised?'; in short, questions relating to the organisation of communication and the media. The questions extended to institutional and administrative considerations of these structures; indeed, in the bibliographies of these works, the great reports by the Council of Europe, UNESCO or the European Broadcasting Union are given a high priority. An example of writing from this period is a work published by Hachette in Paris, but written by two Belgians, one a public service broadcasting director, the other a researcher at the Free University of Brussels (Wangermée and Lhoest 1973).[8] Works covering the press, broadcasting, cinema, theatre and advertising could also be cited.

This issue did not completely disappear after 1980, although it definitely diminished, being superseded by another, more dominant issue. From this point on, it was less a question of how the media and communication should be organised, and more a case of finding out how people and organisations could organise themselves by using communication. Seen from this perspective, communication became a resource, an imperative, an essential route for all those wanting to find a solution to organisational, professional or personal problems. Control communication, it was felt, and problems would cease.

In some ways, power over communication passed from administrative and legal expertise to professional or scientific expertise.
The institutional reports which were such an important part of
bibliographies from works of the 1970s largely disappeared from
subsequent bibliographies. The media and communication were
no longer so important as a technique, their importance resided
elsewhere. From then on, 'the fact of communicating well' became
all-important.

THE HALO EFFECT

The passion for communication and the development of investment in non-material communication resources (both of these a
cause and an effect of the growth of communication discourses,
knowledge and beliefs) together generated a halo effect if we
consider the fields of recruitment and education. In the case of
the former, examples include the errors, if not exaggerations,
in the prediction of jobs and opportunities available within the
communication industry; in the latter, the chaos of university
decision-taking (notably in France) showed the extent to which
the judgement of those in charge of education policy had been
affected by communication discourse.

This obsession with communication and the concurrent development of non-material investment and recruitment draws our attention principally to those milieux concerned with communication
education and research.

In a recent article, the French historian Antoine de Baecque
(1992) argues that intellectuals have not been doing their work.
According to him, the agenda of academics and researchers is
governed more and more by the media, and communication
events; he observes that

> the intellectual has transformed himself into an 'intelligent com-
> mentator' on the texts and images of others. . . . What in the
> past was a platform for ideas has little by little become the main
> site of intellectual endeavour, the open book in which one must
> read the ideas of the times.

He finishes by stating that 'It is in a library one wishes to meet
intellectuals, not on a TV screen.'

In our view, if the intrusion of media reality into theoretical
preoccupations is to be understood positively, topicality cannot be

the only motivating element in the agenda of researchers. Despite the benefits that topicality provides, researchers should not mix solely with professionals or those who, based upon their experience (or their perceptions of their experience), claim an expertise in communication. Professionals cannot realistically be expected to see the return to texts or the opening up of new fields of knowledge as a necessity. Examples of this situation are already evident in the bibliographies of books and courses currently emerging from professional and academic milieux; if the former are content to cite their peers or their specialised communication knowledge, the boldness of the latter lies in their desire to explore a much vaster scientific and theoretical knowledge. While the methodological 'equipment' of the academics is more suited to this endeavour, their intellectual aspirations are, moreover, undeniably far greater.

A striking example of this situation is provided by the sector of organisational communication. Here most public relations manuals (produced within a generally pragmatic sphere) are content to reproduce and reaffirm the comments of previous manuals. Their authors forget that it is often useful to consider how the subject is to be conceptualised, and that they do not have to adhere strictly to their own field of expertise.

TOWARDS A BETTER UNDERSTANDING OF COMMUNICATION KNOWLEDGE AND BELIEFS

A better understanding of the mechanisms by which communication discourses are produced and their effects and contexts is consequently a necessity not only if communication teaching and research is to be improved but also if we are to recognise the many players in the field of communication. For professionals and practitioners too, the situation is a gamble (too many beliefs, too many myths, too many 'corporatisms', above all too many strategies distinguished by the occupation from which they originate).

Other effects may result from the collective passion for communication (itself a product of the multiplication of communication discourses and their valorisation and legitimation), for example, the way in which teachers and researchers are driven to 'mediatise' themselves, on occasions swiftly assuming the role of communication professional themselves. They are beginning to seek the answers to communication questions in communication itself; a testament to this phenomenon can be found in the substantial number of books now being published (and perhaps in course notes also) whose bibliographies are almost uniquely made up of lists of communication books and manuals – without recourse to any social science methodology. This undoubtedly has profound implications for the teaching and structure of communication education.

In conclusion, we feel that an understanding of communication beliefs and knowledge will help all those involved in communication, not only in clarifying their roles and the present context of communication beliefs, but also in allowing them to reflect on the necessary links between theoretical and practical discourses; up to now, these discourses have either been irredeemably separate or, in contrast, too rapidly assimilated into each other (a cloning effect, brought about by an over-concentration on a single, communal pot of beliefs). There is in this increased understanding hope for a 'refinement' of current approaches to communication, the effects of which in the area of education are considerable.

NOTES

This chapter was translated by Dominic Moody.

1 The author subscribes to the hypothesis that during the 1960s and 1970s works relating to linguistics, cybernetics, social anthropology and semiology were not necessarily held to be relevant to the 'field of communication' and, with the exception of some specialists, were not perceived as such. The very homogeneous nature of bibliographies in books declaring themselves to be 'explicitly dedicated to communication' is, at least in part, testimony to this fact, as was the insularity of bookshop and library shelves.
2 See in particular '*Dire L'Entreprise*', special edition of the journal *Reflets et perspectives de la vie économique*, March 1990.
3 This knowledge will either be comprehensive or more superficial, according to the audience.
4 We will not dwell on the quality of the works cited, nor the identity of their quite well-known author.
5 Even if it can be thought that a number of these 'explanations' are motivated more by the desire of the individuals to legitimise their acts.
6 '*Dir-com*' is the corporate, colloquial French term used to describe the class (or clique, or clan) of organisational communication directors, principally within the private sector.
7 Of course, occasionally large material investments continue to be made,

although they are generally proportionally less significant than the effort put into teaching, research and employment (this, at least, is the basis of our 'intuitive hypothesis', since we have not been able to gather the figures on investment and spending for the different periods considered).

8 This is, moreover, the first work to 'foresee', besides video and satellite, the potential of interest in cable television as a subject of scientific study.

BIBLIOGRAPHY

Baecque, A. de (1992) 'Les intellectuels n'ont pas fait leur boulot', *L'Evénement du Jeudi*, 26 March: 132.

Breton, P. (1991) 'L'idéologie de la communication et l'emprise des médias', in J.-N. Charon, (ed.) *L'état des médias*, Paris: La Découverte/ Médias pouvoirs/CPFJ, pp. 243–7.

Breton, P. and Proulx, S. (1989) *L'explosion de la communication: La naissance d'une nouvelle idéologie*, Paris and Montréal: La Découverte/ Boréal.

Dagnaud, M. (1991) 'Gouverner sous le feu des médias', *Le Débat*, September: 54–62.

Gryspeerdt, A. (1982a) 'Communication sociale et médias: les orientations de la recherche en Belgique', *Les Cahiers de la Communication* 4/5: 326–44.

—— (1982b) 'Pour une réflexion sur l'enseignement des relations publiques: vers une approche plus globale et plus ouverte de l'information et de la communication organisationnelle', *PR Contacts* 6: 15–19.

Hennion, A. (1990) 'De l'étude des médias à l'analyse de la médiation: esquisse d'une problématique', *Médias pouvoirs* 20: 39–52.

Jeanneret, Y. (1991) 'La visite d'entreprise: une situation de communication complexe', *Communication et langages* 87: 93–105.

Laulan, A. (1990) 'La société de communication: une nouvelle religion?', in C. Rivière and A. Piette, (eds) *Nouvelles idoles, nouveaux cultes, dérives de la sacralité*, Paris: L'Harmattan, pp. 143–54.

Levaux, V. (1991) 'Trente-cinq ans de la relations publiques et de communication en Belgique: de la découverte des public relations à l'explosion de la communication', in *Guide des Médias*, Deurne: Kluwer Editorial, pp. Lev. 1–18.

McLuhan, M. and Fiore, Q. (1967) *The Medium is the Massage*, London: Allen Lane, The Penguin Press.

Miège, B. (1990) *La société conquise par la communication*, Grenoble: PUG Grenoble.

Missika, J. (1991) 'Les Français et leurs médias: le désenchantement', *Médias pouvoirs* 21: 97–114.

Neveu, E. and Rieffel, R. (1991) 'Les effets de réalité des sciences de la communication', *Réseaux* 50: 11–40.

Panofsky, E. (1987) *La perspective comme forme symbolique*, Paris: Minuit.

Proulx, S. (1990) 'De la métaphore télégraphique à celle de la conversation: représentations du pouvoir des médias et modèles de la communication', in L. Sfez and G. Coutlée, (eds) *Technologies et symboliques de la communication*, Grenoble: PUG Grenoble, pp. 283–97.

Verhaegen, P. (1990) 'Aspects communicationnels de la transmission des connaissances: le cas de la vulgarisation scientifique', *Recherches Sociologiques* XXI(3): 323–51.

Wangermée, R. and Lhoest, H. (1973) *L'après-télévision, une anti-mythologie de l'audiovisuel*, Paris: Hachette Littérature.

Chapter 12

Teaching communication during an accelerating media evolution
A lifelong learning process?

Klaus Merten

Of all affairs, communication is the most wonderful
(John Dewey)

Teaching communication, of course, is a process of meta-communication and has, as all meta-processes, a genuine power of its own. Furthermore, the teaching of communication with a focus upon the media is dependent upon the state of media effects research.

In this chapter, I first show that the evolution of the media is still in progress. This, of course, influences the effects that the media will have on the recipient. Second, I argue that media education must expand to become communication education; this transformation is due, inevitably, to changes in effects research itself. This provokes some hypotheses which will be presented in the final section.

THE EVOLUTION OF MEDIA

Evolution entails the fulfilment of four conditions: (a) change of structure, (b) in a specific manner, (c) over a period of time, and (d) resulting in an improvement of the structure. This holds true for biological systems as well as for social systems where 'the gene has been replaced by the symbol' (Parsons 1964: 341). In particular, this will hold true for communication, since communication is a basic process which catalyses all higher types of social systems and, at the same time, connects psychological systems. Or, to put it another way: the evolution of communication is a necessary precondition for the evolution of societies. The status of a society's communication increases in an evolutionary manner.

According to Daniel Bell (1976), societies develop according to a three-stage model in which problems concerning the transportation of mass, energy and information are addressed and resolved. The transportation of mass is the main problem of ancient societies. Its solution is the connecting of paths and streets, that is, the application of a communicative principle of connection to the problem of transporting masses: all roads lead to Rome. The second problem arises in modern industrial societies: the transportation of energy. Again, the solution comes from the communicative principle of connection – in this case, pipelines, electricity, laser. The third problem arises in the post-industrial society: the transportation of information. The solution depends on the application of the same principle: connecting wires, channels and paths of communication – telephone, telex, telefax or mail-boxes, for instance. A closer look at this solution shows that this is the application of a communicative structure to communication itself, that is, the installation of a reflexive structure. According to systemic theories (Luhmann 1970; Merten 1977), we know that the installation of reflexive structures catalyses innovative possibilities, and increases efficiency. Or, to put it in another way: reflexivity of communication marks the beginning of the media society.

The consequence of this development can easily be described: communication, in former times only a simple tool accorded little attention by society, is evolving to become the leading societal subsystem: the political system today depends heavily on the power of public opinion; the economic system cannot act without advertising and increasing efforts in public relations. Even the cultural system depends on the media: arts and sports are sponsored by the media, and, of course, all performances of music, opera or theatre are reflected in and by the media. Nothing is real and nothing is relevant unless it is in the media.

THE OBJECT OF MEDIA EDUCATION: MEDIA EFFECTS

The state of media education is the result of a continuous but accelerating change caused by the evolution of the media. Therefore, to describe the state of media education, we must first look to its subject, the media and their effects.

Media education began as the direct result of the film analyses carried out as a part of the famous Payne Fund studies in the 1920s in the United States (Charters 1933). Edgar Dale (1935) carried out a content analysis of films, using ten thematic categories (crime, sex, love, comedy, mystery, war, children, history, travel and social propaganda). From his analysis of a sample of 1,500 films, collected in 1925, 1930 and 1935, he discovered that 75 per cent of all films used only three categories, namely crime, sex and love. These results alarmed the American public and reinforced the 'legacy of fear': 'The commercial movies are an unsavoury mess. . . . "the producers ought to have a heart" over their bad influences on children' (Charters 1933: 54). These and other results inspired Peters (1933) to write a book about how watching films affects morality – probably the first book on media education. About forty years later the same fears arose again, when television programmes entered the scene.

But what really happened? In both cases the following conditions obtained: (a) a new medium began to spread contents (b) which were thought to cause harmful effects to young people and children so that (c) educational efforts concerning the contents and responses to the contents of these media seemed to be urgently needed. The shortcomings of these efforts were overlooked: (a) media effects research was related only to a special medium, not to the whole communication situation, and (b) studies of long-term influences were not yet available, that is: media education was grounded only on a surface structure of supposed fears arising from the presence of the media.

These fears depended mainly on an understanding of the communication process based on the classic stimulus–response model. This model was adapted for communication research by Harold D. Lasswell, one of the four great 'fathers of communication research' (Schramm 1963), so that it could be used for the definition and description of the effects of communication:

> The strategy of propaganda . . . can readily be described in the language of stimulus–response. . . . The propagandist may be said to be concerned with the multiplication of those stimuli which are best calculated to evoke the desired response, and with the nullification of those stimuli which are likely to instigate the undesired response.
>
> (Lasswell 1927: 630)

Later, Schramm criticised this over-simple conceptualisation as follows: 'At that time, the audience was typically thought of as a sitting target; if a communicator could hit it, he would affect it . . .

I have elsewhere called this the bullet theory of mass communication' (Schramm and Roberts 1972: 8).

In summarising the objections against the classical model we must first discuss its basic assumptions of proportionality, causality and transitivity. The shortcomings related to proportionality in the stimulus–response model are easily detected if one considers its semantic aspects, in particular the ascription of meaning to any stimulus, which is only possible on the supposition that there is a strictly denotative meaning that is the same for all recipients. When Mowrer (1954: 663) defines communication as a 'transfer of meaning', he is taking this type of fixed meaning for granted.

However, communication depends not on signals but on symbols. That is, the meaning of a symbol is not denotative, but connotative, structured and subject to change according to the communication situation. The development of language might not have been possible had humans not employed arbitrary, digital coding on their utterances (Ekman and Friesen 1969: 60), and this, necessarily, implies selectivity.

And it is selectivity which is in operation across the whole communication process: from attention to perception, from remembering to uttering sentences (see, e.g., Broadbent 1958; Krippendorff 1989; Sanders 1963). It is to be expected that this strategic concept operates not only in the communication process but also in the process of effects.

Causality, the second assumption inherent in the stimulus–response model, imposes a temporal structure in relating causes and effects. But causality is imputed as a structure by humans on the basis of experience, it is by no means a law. In effects research, however, we cannot impute causality. For, as the concept of selectivity suggests, there may be many effects sharing a single cause and many causes for the same effect.

Orson Welles's famous broadcast of 'The War of the Worlds' in 1938 has often been cited as evidence for strong media effects in the sense of the classical stimulus–response model. But a closer look suggests another explanation. According to the study by Cantril et al. (1947), the structure of the effects process runs as follows: People who turned on the radio in the evening of the broadcast heard about an attack from Mars. The great majority did not believe the content, but a minority became anxious enough to turn to the telephone for reassurance. Because so many people were ringing up the police and broadcasting stations, telephone lines were jammed. So some of these very people jumped to another false interpretation, which made quite good sense according to William and Dorothy Thomas's 'definition of the situation-theorem' (Thomas and Thomas 1932: 572). In short, this theorem says that once people have defined a situation – rightly or wrongly – they tend to maintain their interpretation. The interpretation of the anxious people was: the telephones are not jammed because they are busy, they are out of action because of actual damage by the invaders from Mars. Therefore, these people became panic-stricken, ran out of their houses and drove off in their cars.

At that moment, then, they served as model for the behaviour of others and were copied by them. If this modelling function of others – as, for instance, Ash's famous experiments (1951) show – is strong enough, people can behave wholly irrationally. In case of perceived danger to life, people, as panic research tells us (Quarantelli 1978), are apt to define a situation according to the Thomas theorem as a situation of actual danger. What was really in operation and reinforcing was a principle of social imitation – to do what others do, to share a common perception and interpretation: a systemic, reflexive and most powerful structure was at work.

The same holds true for a widely known and powerful effect in communication, namely the imputing of a comment or an opinion to a message. As one can show (Merten 1977), this is to impute to information an extra layer of meaning, it is meta-information. Attitudes, as a further example, can be defined as filters for the selection of available information on the meta-level, and are, therefore, to be considered as another type of reflexive structure. These are powerful mechanisms.

The catalogue of effects, then, shows many types of reflexive structure, and this holds true especially for strong effects. For example, in bandwagon and underdog effect research (Fleitas 1971; Simon 1954), or in the process of opinion formation by the spiral of silence (Noelle-Neumann 1989), or in other theories of opinion change, we will always detect such types of reflexive structure. Therefore, it seems evident that not causal, but reflexive, structures are the decisive structures which account for effects.

Transitivity means – according to physics – that, to have an effect, there must be some kind of transfer from a source to a recipient – this is the assumption of the classical stimulus–response model. But again, the analogy between physics and communication science proved to be only epiphenomenal, not substantial: in the communication process, there is nothing to be transferred unchanged from a communicator to a recipient. Therefore, all types of transitive assumptions – one way or symmetric – are misleading.

Communication, then, is not a process of single or symmetric transfer of information; instead, it is an asymmetric process by which a communicator offers some information and a recipient makes a selection from it. Elements of the message are shared and made common to both, communicator and recipient, but the multiple and pervasive selective behaviour of the recipient thoroughly contradicts the assumption of transitivity.

One gains further support for this position from the findings of constructivist research. According to Maturana and Varela (1979), there is no copy of a 'real' objective reality in our brain. Therefore, we construct our reality in a fully subjective manner by selecting from any communication offer some pieces, put them together with external pieces of relevant contexts and internal, personal experience, thereby constructing our information and our subjective reality. In the same sense, constructivists deny any type of objective reality and allow, at the best, an intersubjective reality (Foerster 1979; Krippendorff 1989; Varela 1984). From this point of view, the assumption of transitivity in the effects process is completely misleading, since transitivity presupposes an objective reality, in which some type of information in the communicator's brain can be transferred identically into the brain of the recipient.

Therefore, in place of the assumption of transivitity in the effect process, we prefer to substitute the assumption of constructivity, assuming that every brain has a degree of freedom to select from every information offer.

Summing up, the basic assumptions of the classical stimulus–response model cannot be valid. The recipient cannot be thought of as a defenceless victim who is aimed at and hit continuously by omnipotent stimulus guns (Schramm 1954: 3ff.): the theory of strong effects was first thrown into doubt by the findings of Lazarsfeld et al. (1948) in Erie county and must now be ruled out – at least theoretically.

Bearing this in mind, in the final section we shall attempt to summarise these positions and outline an alternative model based on a systemic approach to communication.

We infer that there are no stimuli at work which cause effects.

Instead, we suppose that any 'communication' provides the recipient with an information offer, from which he or she selects pieces according to some selective criteria. These selective criteria may be external and/or internal. External criteria are provided by the situational context in which the proper message is embedded and which may be differentiated according to temporal, social and/or objective dimensions (Luhmann 1981; Merten 1977).

In the temporal perspective whether, for instance, the message is a new one or is a repetition of something already known by the recipient is of utmost importance for the possible effect. The news value of any piece of information, then, is not a property of the message itself, but a type of external and/or internal context, generated by the presence of the message and the recipient's past experience of it.

In the social perspective, the effect of the message becomes heavily over-structured, for instance, by the presence of others who may act as models, as Asch's famous experiments (1951) have widely demonstrated.

In the objective perspective, every type of meta-information, for instance commentaries or other evaluative remarks presented in association with the message, will act selectively on the proper message, thereby changing the 'proper' effect of the message.

Internal selective criteria are structured very similarly: in the temporal respect, all types of experience provide anchors, built up in the past. Expectancies are another form of this structure.

In the social dimension, the anticipation of the actions of others provides valuable criteria for the processing of information offers, as the theory of symbolic interaction has shown (Horton and Wohl 1956).

In the objective dimension, all types of attitudes, which are centred on norms or values, act as selective criteria, and influence decisions about the selection from the information offers possible.

To generalise these considerations: the effect of a message depends probably only to a minor extent on the message itself but is influenced to a major extent by the external and/or internal contexts.

Summing up: the effects process is based on selectivity instead of proportionality, reflexivity instead of causality and constructivity instead of transitivity. The effect of any message, therefore, is by no means to be grasped from the message itself but is built up as a trimodal construction of the message and an external and internal context, which over-structure the proper message, building up an internal information (in a constructivistic sense) that changes the actual internal context (knowledge, attitudes, etc.).

Formalized, the trimodal model specifies any effect as

$$\text{EFFECT} = f\ (M_{\text{essage}}\ E_{\text{xt. context}}\ I_{\text{nt. context}})$$

There is a further highly relevant feature of this model. Any new information offer will cause a change in the internal storage of knowledge, attitudes, etc. But in the same moment, if the internal context controls any input, the probability is that the internal context will lead to changes in any further effect process thereby changing the internal context itself.

The same may hold true on the social level: if the media – as we suppose – are strong agents of social change, social change will, in turn, affect media contents, media consumption and, finally, media effects.

> We have seen . . . a number of seemingly convincing generalizations about media effects that may have been valid in their time. As new media were widely adopted and as our society developed new habits of using mass communication, those generalizations become obsolete and untrustworthy. . . . Thus, as society and the media change, their effects can be expected to change.
>
> (Lowery and De Fleur 1983: 360)

Summarising, this leads to the thesis that *effects will change further effects*. Finally, if we remember that effects are defined as a change in knowledge and/or attitude and/or behaviour (Katz and Lazarsfeld 1955: 19), this thesis may be read as *changes change changes*.

FROM MEDIA EDUCATION TO COMMUNICATION EDUCATION

Teaching communication, then, is a process subject to three major types of change. These depend on the evolution of communication. First, new media are appearing continuously and widen the communication scene in two ways. Not only are they being used in themselves but their competitive and complementary relation to other media is of the utmost interest. That is, we cannot describe the influence of a specific medium without the context of all other available media and communication facilities.

Second, as shown above, effects of media are not fixed according to a nomological theory irrespective of time and region; instead, they vary according to different media, to the amount of media available and, last but not least, in the temporal respect.

Third, social change changes the mentalities of people; their interests, their sensibilities and their norms and values change. In any one year, harmful or damaging effects may result from receiving media contents but this may not be the case in any subsequent year.

Putting these three factors together, teaching communication becomes a little like the work of the ancient Sysiphus: what can be learned today about the proper use and the effects of communication may have vanished tomorrow,[1] and this process is accelerating.

The effects of communication are changing due to the development of new communication facilities. Therefore, teaching communication cannot be helpful if it works on the basis of a static 'today': no catalogue of valid knowledge will ever be available. Teaching communication has a chance if it can itself be structured as a continuous process of change: it must make a proper use of trends in the development of knowledge about the effects of communication. And it must further take into account that it will no longer suffice to look at the impact of a single medium in order to understand effects. Instead, it will always be necessary to study the effects of a single medium in relation to the whole pattern of communication available at that time. Or, to put it in another way: media education must be replaced by communication education.

NOTE

1 This holds true if one considers that effects research itself has a time lag of about ten years before it can be fruitfully employed in teaching communications.

REFERENCES

Asch, Solomon E. (1951) 'Effects of group pressure upon the modification and distortion of judgements', in Harald Guetzkow (ed.) *Groups, Leadership and Men*, Pittsburgh, PA: Carnegie Press, pp. 177–90.

Bell, Daniel (1976) 'Welcome to the post-industrial society', *Physics Today* 29.

Broadbent, Daniel E. (1958) *Perception and Communication*, Oxford: Pergamon Press.

Campbell, Donald T. (1969) 'Variation and selective retention in socio-cultural evolution', *General Systems* 14: 69–85.

Cantril, Hadley, Gaudet, Hazel and Herzog, Herta (1947) *The Invasion from Mars: A Study of the Psychology of Panic*, Princeton, NJ: Princeton University Press.

Charters, W. W. (1933) *Motion Picture and Youth: A Summary*, New York: Macmillan.

Dale, Edgar (1935) *The Content of Motion Pictures*, New York: Macmillan.

Ekman, Paul and Friesen, Wallace V. (1969) 'The repertoire of non-verbal behaviour: categories, origins, usage, and coding', *Semiotica* 1: 49–98.

Fleitas, Daniel W. (1971) 'Bandwaggon and underdog effects in minimal information-elections', *American Political Science Review*, 65: 434–8.

Foerster, Heinz von (1979) *Observing Systems*, Seaside: Intersystems.

Horton, O. and Wohl, R. R. (1956) 'Mass communication and para-social interaction', *Psychiatry* 19: 215–29.

Katz, Elihu and Lazarsfeld, Paul F. (1955) *Personal Influence*, Glencoe, IL: Free Press.

Krippendorff, Klaus (1989) 'On the ethics of constructing communication', in Brenda Dervin, Lawrence Grossberg, Barbara J. O'Keefe and Ellen Wartberg (eds) *Rethinking Communication*, vol. 1, Newbury Park, CA, and London: Sage, pp. 66–96.

Lasswell, Harold D. (1927) 'The theory of political propaganda', *American Political Science Review* 21: 627–31.

Lazarsfeld, Paul F., Berelson, Bernard and Gaudet, Hazel (1948) *The People's Choice*, New York: Columbia Press.

Lowery, Shearon and De Fleur, Melvin (1983) *Milestones in Mass Communication Research*, New York and London: Longman.

Luhmann, Niklas (1970) 'Reflexive Mechanismen', in *Soziologische Aufklärung*, Opladen: Westdeutscher Verlag, pp. 92–112.

—— (1981) 'The improbability of communication', *Social Science Journal* 23: 122–32.

Maturana, Humberto R. and Varela, F. J. (1979) *Autopoiesis and Cognition: Boston Studies in the Philosophy of Science*, Boston, MA: Reidel.

Merten, Klaus (1977) 'Reflexivity in human communication', *Communication Yearbook* 1: 121–32.

Mowrer, O. H. (1954) 'The psychologist looks at language', *American Psychologist* 9: 660–94.

Noelle-Neumann, Elisabeth (1989) *The Spiral of Silence: Public Opinion – Our Social Skin*, Chicago, IL, and London: University of Chicago Press.

Parsons, Talcott (1964) 'Evolutionary universals in society', *American Sociological Review* 29: 339–57.

Peters, Charles C. (1933) *Motion Pictures and Standards of Morality*, New York: Macmillan.

Quarantelli, Enrico L. (ed.) (1978) *Disasters: Theory and Research*, Beverley Hills, CA, and London: Sage.

Sanders, Andries, F. (1963) *The Selective Process in the Functional Visual Field*, Assen: Van Gorcum.

Schramm, Wilbur (ed.) (1954) *The Process and Effects of Mass Communication*, Urbana: University of Illinois Press, pp. 3–26.

Schramm, Wilbur (1963) *The Science of Human Communication*, New York: Basic Books.

Schramm, Wilbur and Roberts, Donald F. (eds) (1972) *The Process and Effects of Mass Communication*, rev. edn, Urbana, Chicago and London: University of Illinois Press.

Simon, Herbert A. (1954) 'Bandwaggon and underdog effects and the possibility of election prediction', *Public Opinion Quarterly* 18: 245–53.

Thomas, William I. and Thomas, Dorothy S. (1932) *The Child in America*, New York: Knopf.

Varela, F. (1984) 'Two principles for self-organization', in H. Ulrich and J. B. Probst (eds) *Self-organization and Management of Social Systems*, New York: Springer, pp. 25–32.

Chapter 13

Teaching and linguistic research on 'communication and media'

Jeanne-Marie Barberis

Without claiming to give an overall view of all the complex components and tendencies in media teaching today in France, as a
lecturer at Paul Valéry University (Montpellier III) and a member
of PRAXILING (DIPRALANG research team) I can draw upon
my own experience as a university teacher and researcher in a
given discipline, linguistics, to illustrate an aspect of communication and media teaching in France.

The legitimacy of my participation in this collective work on
the media rests entirely upon the recent theoretical and methodological propositions in linguistics, particularly in the field of oral
expression, and analysis of verbal interaction and conversation.
Linguistics has made considerable progress these last few years
by managing to shake off abstraction and hidebound formalism –
formalism which forbade the analyst from taking any interest in
the communication context, the relations of language with referen-
tial reality, and even authentic interactions, in favour of examples
concocted by the researcher.

Having worked for several years on the media and more generally on the functioning of speech in interviews, I have tried to
draw up a few observations from the study of these phenomena,
and place them within the theoretical framework of the linguistic
analysis of oral expression. The interview analysis developed later
in the paper is an example of the research work that takes place in
our department and the type of teaching we undertake.

RESEARCH WORK AND UNIVERSITY TEACHING

The praxematic linguistics group (PRAXILING) started off as a
research group set up in the 1980s. It has elaborated a method for

the textual analysis of written expression and also participated in the recent development of oral discourse analysis. The study of the media according to this dual linguistic approach (analysis of written expression and of oral interaction) is taught at all university levels (mainly first and second cycle – i.e. to MA level – but also third cycle: postgraduate) within the framework of the Language Sciences Department. The teaching is oriented towards an approach which is both linguistic and, more generally, communicative (communication strategies and techniques, characteristics of public discourse, mass communication, interview structure and analysis). For the moment all this only constitutes a thematic option which is not institutionalised and does not lead to a specific diploma centred on the media. It may be noted, however, that the Language Sciences Department obtained for the university year beginning 1991 the authorisation from the Education Ministry to set up a DEUG (two-year undergraduate programme) in 'Communication and Language Sciences'.

COMMUNICATION AND MEDIA AT MONTPELLIER III: A BRIEF DESCRIPTION

The 'communication and media' section does not at present have any officially institutionalised existence at Paul Valéry University. In the Arts and Human Sciences Faculty, there are two sections which carry out the teaching (first and second cycle, as well as some in the third cycle) devoted to the media: the Language Sciences Department, centred on a linguistic and communicative approach, and the ISAV (Image, Sound, Audiovisual) section, oriented towards aesthetics and the performing arts (cinema, theatre, music, radio, television).

The absence of a single, coherent teaching structure for mass communication at Paul Valéry is the result of the fragmentation of disciplines, and of the weight of tradition within each discipline, where media communication means something different for each.

The phenomenon is far from unique to Paul Valéry University, and can be found in many French universities, as well as outside the university structure. For example, the professional training of journalists is done in Journalism Schools, not in universities.

At the national level, this disparateness is faithfully reflected by the National University Committee, the body which evaluates university teachers, and within which their various disciplines are supposed to be represented. There are at least three sections dealing with media communication:

- Section 7: Language Sciences (linguistics and general phonetics);
- Section 18: The Plastic and Performing Arts (music, aesthetics, art theory);
- Section 71: Information and Communication Sciences.

Sociology (Section 19) should also be added to the list, for it has shown great interest in the media, especially in their impact on public opinion. Moreover, certain sociologists and anthropologists have put forward some decisive notions concerning communication analysis (particularly Bateson and Goffman).

In this chapter I shall describe a project from the linguistics side, although other disciplines are also developing teaching and research on the media. The analysis which follows illustrates the type of research and teaching we undertake based on perspectives drawn from linguistics.

FROM PROFFERED SPEECH TO REPRESENTED SPEECH: THE MEDIA AND THE POLITICIAN'S IMAGE

The power of words: slogans' names and the politician's image

During his first seven-year term of office, the President of the French Republic, François Mitterrand, by popular consent, was affably dubbed 'Tonton' (an affectionate diminutive for 'uncle'). In a similar way, he has recently been given another sobriquet (which dates from the beginning of his second term of office): 'God'. And the Press has been rife with comments on the ups and downs of the 'divine' moods of the President, especially in regard to journalists.

On a semantic level, these two nicknames are in harmony with the image that the President sought to display during his first campaign in 1981, through the political slogan: 'The tranquil force'. 'Tonton' and 'God': in both cases, force and authority; in both cases, calm and distance. But the irony of the second nickname turns it into the inverse of the first. It sanctions a feeling of distance between the President and the people he administers – a distance immeasurably greater for a god than an uncle.

I want to introduce here the problem of the politician's image.

The approach-distance analysis grid allows us to symbolise the rituals which regulate the social distances between individuals, in the interactions of daily life (conversation), but also in more formal occasions, such as the interview of a politician on television. A president today has to 'step into the arena' in order to defend his image: he has to put it back into play by exposing himself to journalists' questions. The game played here is the interview. To illustrate the use of linguistics I shall examine a short extract from a television interview given by Monsieur Mitterrand in March 1988. Already the incumbent President of the Republic, he announces at the beginning of the interview his intention to seek a second mandate, though not without having maintained a well-publicised suspense for a long time: in spite of being harassed by journalists, it was only thirty-three days before the presidential election that he agreed to answer – with a 'yes' – the question 'are you a candidate?' This was after tension has been aroused in the media and in public opinion, and the irritation of his rivals had mounted (as long as his candidature had not been officially announced, they were only potential rivals, and could not truly attack him).

The political interview can undoubtedly lend itself to various approaches. My point of view is that of a linguist. More exactly, I shall put forward some reflections in the field that linguists call verbal interaction analysis, or conversation analysis: this is a field in which the praxematic linguistics group (PRAXILING) has been working for some ten years. In order to clarify the status of speech (by which I mean oral expression), it is useful to study how it is managed in the interview exchange (discourse strategies, position of the actors).

Interview of François Mitterrand (F.M.), 22 March 1988, Antenne 2 News, 8 p.m.

Journalists: Henri Sannier (H.S.), Paul Amar (P.A.)

Conventions of the transcription:
The participants are identified by their initials, H.S., F.M., P.A., and the answers numbered in their order of appearance.
Slashes /, //, ///, indicate the length of pauses.
Colons :, ::, :::, indicate a lengthening of syllables.
h, hh = inhalation. Variation : mh, mhh : inhalation with initial occlusion.
t, tt = clicking of tongue.
Capital letter: strong attack on the initial syllable.
An apostrophe indicates contracted syllables.
Word or fragment bracketed by the figure (2): loud voice, emphasis.
? = rising intonation.
! = emphatic intonation.
The length of the pause between two utterances is indicated at the beginning of the second utterance between parentheses.
Any extra features (laugh, cough, peculiarities of speech) appear between parentheses in italics.

Transcription of the beginning of the interview:

French	English
French	*English*
H.S.1 – ma première question est simple et: directe à la fois / vous allez le voir quelque chose me dit d'ailleurs que: que je s'rai le: / le dernier journaliste de france et de navarre hh à vous poser cette question m'sieur le président? hh êtes-vous un nouveau candidat? / tt à la présidence de la république F.M.2 – (2.5) m oui? P.A.3 – mhh vous avez:: mûrement réfléchi? F.M.4 – (2.) je l'crois H.S.5 – on peut savoir (2) quand (2) vous avez pris cette décision	H.S.1 – my first question is simple and: direct at the same time / you'll see that something tells me in fact that: that I'll be the: / the last journalist from france or anywhere hh to ask you this question mister president? hh are you a candidate again? / tt for the presidency of the republic F.M.2 – (2.5) m yes? P.A.3 – mhh have you:: given it due consideration? F.M.4 – (2.) I think so H.S.5 – may we know (2) when (2) you took this decision some

certains disent c'est en juillet quatre-vingt-sept d'aut' disent c'est pendant les fêtes de fin d'année?

F.M.6 – je n'en sais rien moi-même (*sing-song voice*)

P.A.7 – hh au fond pourquoi:: briguez-vous un second mandat monsieur le président j'allais dire / monsieur le candidat

F.M.8 – (2.5) hh vous savez depuis euh // t déjà:: // tt quelques mois: / mhh j'ai (2) Beaucoup' (2) écouté: les discours des unz' et des autres / mhh et dans Tout ce bruit: j'aperçois un risque pour le pays: / mhh de retomber dans les: querelles et les divisions qui si souvent: / h l'ont Miné / eh bien je veux / que la france / soit unie // et elle ne le sera pas: ! // hh si euh: / elle est prise en main par euh / des esprits:: / intolérants / par: des: partis: qui veulent Tout // par des Clans // ou par des Bandes

say it was in july eighty-seven others say it w's during the end of year celebrations?

F.M.6 – I have no idea myself (*sing-song voice*)

P.A.7 – hh deep down why:: are you seeking a second mandate mister president I was going to say / mister candidate

F.M.8 – (2.5) hh you know that for uh // t already now:: // tt a few months: / mhh I've (2) been listening: a Lot (2) to what this or that person has been saying / mhh and in All this noise: I can see a risk for the country: / mhh of falling back into the: quarrels and divisions which so often: / h have underMined it / well I want / france / to be united // and it won't be: ! // hh if uh: / it is taken over by uh / intolerant / minds:: / by parties: which want Everything // by Clans // or by Groups

Analysis of the interview

In order to speak, but also in order to interpret the speech of others, we are subject to conventionalised images of speech. The use of speech is constantly constrained by conventionalised representations of speech.

This is so, first, because all human interaction is stamped with theatricality: there are pre-established roles; there is a stage, where the social show that has been prepared is put on; and wings where the preparations for the show are kept hidden. There are masks for the characters: each must produce an acceptable façade for his partners, and woe betide he or she who 'loses face'.

An interaction is also subject to rituals, to an almost religious ceremonial, in which certain protagonists approach others as if making an offer to a beneficiary. Care and respect must be shown between protagonists.

In this theatrical production and interaction ritual, certain elements are rejected, not into the wings, but into an area not noticed by speakers and listeners: there exist mainly unconscious processes which play a part in the elaboration of the meaning of a scene without the participants' knowledge. Among these unconscious meanings,[1] we find those which have often been grouped under the label 'body language': gestures, facial expressions, looks, the occupation of space (proxemics). More generally speaking, the way in which language is – unconsciously – enacted by the body is one of the matrices of the representation of speech.

Presentation, formality and ritualisation of the exchange

A biased communication

It is well-known that audiovisual communication is a biased communication – the speaker of a televised message addresses absent listeners, who can see without being seen. This is especially apparent when the message is addressed 'face to face' to the viewer. This message is a tripartite interaction, of which the addressee remains, of course, the television viewer, but where the communication show is inserted within another communication: that of the television medium with the public.

The spatial presentation of the interaction

Several spatial schemata are used in the case of this interview with Mitterrand to frame the actors present: the participants are seen in profile, with the viewer witnessing their total face to face position, or the camera switches back and forth between alternate frontal views or three-quarter profile views of protagonists. The choice here is mainly of frames which highlight the President, who is seen alone on the screen, face on. More rarely, the camera moves to an image of the two journalists who are interviewing him; but he is seen in three-quarter frontal profile rather than fully face on; occasionally the two journalists appear in three-quarter profile: this conveys the meaning that they are addressing the President, whereas the frontal framing of the President is intended to make us believe that he is looking at the viewer opposite him. In fact the predominant strategy consisted in placing the camera behind the two journalists, but without them being visible. The advantage is that Mitterrand looks straight ahead in a manner that is natural. He seems to be looking to the viewer, whereas in fact he is looking at his interlocutors. However, the President's eyes can be seen moving from one to the other of the two unseen interlocutors, in synchronisation with the speakers' turn-taking (slight but clear sideways eye movements).

A highly constructed communication

The speakers speak more for the viewer than for their apparent interlocutor, knowing that the quality of their media image will depend on the quality of their interactive performance. We can see, as a result, some interesting elocution phenomena, which show the specificity of this highly constructed communication, as opposed to 'natural' conversations, or even to more informal media events (chat shows, for example).

First of all, verbal marks of retroaction within other speakers' turns, such as (hm, hm), (yes),[2] are totally absent in this interview: there is no 'back channel' because the interactants are not free to jointly take charge of their message. It is not just a matter between themselves, and Mitterrand is in no way talking to convince his interlocutors, but to convince the viewers. Neither can we find the speaker soliciting agreement with expressions (like *you see? eh?* or question tags) which provide an opportunity habitually offered by the speaker to allow the interlocutor to react positively via the back channel. The synchronisation of the exchange is therefore weak. Some internal effects of the President-journalist interaction are noticeable, however: the interviewer's ironic *vous avez:: mûrement réflechi? (have you:: given it due consideration?)* (in the particular context in which everybody knew that the President had deferred adopting any position about his possible candidature for another presidential mandate), a fleeting irony in the quickness of the exchange, seems for internal use rather than for the public.

Next, Mitterrand's elocution is more that of a public figure making a declaration than of a protagonist in a conversation. In this respect, we can oppose the interviewer's more rapid and natural elocution to Mitterrand's words, which are carefully considered (slow delivery, hesitation markers and frequent pauses) and rhetorically underlined (strong attack of initial syllables, studied rhythms like the ternary rhythm: *eh bien je veux / que la*

france / soit unie (well I want / France / to be united) to strengthen
the argumentation. Similarly, the numerous marked intakes of
breath correspond more to the speaker's tension (psychological
tension but also physical tension due to the necessity of strongly
proffered speech) than to the fluency of everyday speech.

Finally, because of the preparation that goes into this sort of
media ceremony, the questions and answers sound like quotations,
like 'pre-signalled' messages, as in the case of the interviewer's
*monsieur le président j'allais dire / monsieur le candidat (mister
president I was going to say / mister candidate).* Mitterrand's first
three answers seem quite strange in intonation. The *oui?* on a
rising intonation (therefore quite uncharacteristic of an
affirmation), after a pout which is both a pout of faked hesitation
(a facial expression of hesitation which is sometimes sounded as
mmm, barely audible in the case we are dealing with) and a teasing
pout, is at odds with the convinced tone of the candidate in his
declaration of candidacy. In the third answer, the sing-song on the
last three syllables (a higher pitch on the *moi*) again makes
the intonation curve atypical of a simple declaration. Mitterrand's
answers are preceded by long reaction times. All this is at the
opposite extremity to the rapid surge of speech – these elocution
phenomena, in so far as they correspond to an exchange ritualisation, lead us towards a larger, more global field of interpretation:
the symbolic positions of the interactants in this type of tightly
controlled and very well-prepared face to face interaction.

The ritualisation of the exchange

There are two interconnected effects here: the public figure's for-
mality and strict control of his speech, and the exercise of his
power over the message, in the direction both of the journalists
and of the viewers. In fact, Mitterrand is merely prolonging his
strategy right up to the end: he 'makes us wait', he distils
his syllables with parsimony, accompanying them with the sibylline
smile of an oracle. What is going on here is a symbolic taking
of power, which can be interpreted as follows: every individual
possesses a territory. Among his assets, his personal goods, there
is the time he has in which to speak, and more especially in which
to answer questions (just as there is a time which people may be
made to wait at appointments, variable according to the power of
the person who makes others wait). The very answer which the

President is asked to give is an encroachment upon his territory: he 'holds' the answer, which is part of his private domain; moreover, and especially, to answer the question is to commit himself for the future, since by saying *yes* or *no* he sets the seal on a decision of importance. For someone with power, the answer can either not be given (a strategy which will be used later in the same interview, to skirt round a question on nationalisation and on the candidate's programme), or be deferred or ambiguous, or be given lip service only and delivered without conviction. That, at least, is one of the strategies possible: a conservation strategy, of a territorial kind. The speaker in this case calls upon his 'negative face', as described by Brown and Levinson (1978) (following Goffman 1967, who himself drew his inspiration from Durkheim [1915]).

Social relations are regulated here both within the interview interaction (President-journalists relation) and within the communication between the television medium and the viewers. They follow rituals based on positivity (approach rituals, signalling a 'movement towards the other') or negativity (rituals of avoidance, signalling a retreat into one's own sphere and the wish to defend one's territory and maintain distance from others).

We have here a first explanation of the nickname which emerged from people's talk during the second term of office: 'God'. Mitterrand's reserved attitude, both benign and distant, signifies a demand for 'deference'. This demand is of a negative type: it calls upon rites of avoidance, which are based upon prohibition. The 'ideal sphere' which the individual draws around himself, and which constitutes his domain, becomes vast and maintains others at a great and respectful distance. Power leads to remoteness, and the remoteness increases the longer one stays in power. These rites are connected to the sacred: the inaccessibility is that of the idol and the impenetrable space which surrounds him, as described by Durkheim in *Elementary Forms of Religious Life* (1915).

Maintenance of a social image and corporal transfix

An individual, in his or her professional behaviour, for example, tends to adopt a 'middle position' expressed by a habitus, a way of being, which is maintained like a guiding thread over and beyond the variations due to circumstances. Sales staff, for example, must permanently display 'friendliness' (smiling, enthusiasm). And what of a president? And a journalist?

The difference between the two interviewers, Sannier and Amar, is quite marked. The former strongly maintains a smile as a corporal transfix during interviews, whereas Amar's attitude is more reserved.

Mitterrand is sparing in gestures and movements. His transfix-expression amounts to a very slight smile, distant. This habit signifies a 'withdrawal' position, a territorial strategy rather than one of approach. We see here the strategic position which has already been noted in connection with the President's interactional attitude during the interview. Here there is no doubt a second explanation of the 'divine' character to which the President has been assimilated. The static and reserved nature of the body expression signifies the maintenance of a power, through what Christian Rolot calls, in his study of politicians' television performances, a conservation strategy (as opposed to conquest strategies: Rolot 1986; Rolot and Ramirez 1988). Candidates already 'in place', like Mitterrand, tend to use the first, and the challengers, the outsiders, the second. But there are important variations in the interpretation of these two types of role according to individuals and temperaments. At any rate, Mitterrand's distant smile is indeed a transfix, as we see him, during certain interviews, severely attack the Press and the journalists present, while continuing to smile. . . .

The image which is thus projected via the body habitus has of course a 'natural' base (one's 'temperament'). But once this image is isolated, it is worked upon, and perfected, on the initiative of the candidate as well as his communication advisers. It grows into a reified character, to the point where, when the symbol takes precedence over substance, a feeling of unreality emerges from these pictures, which become extremely rigid.

In the same way that the meaning of words can become fixed and rigid to the point where they only convey stereotypes, there would seem to be, then, a reification of meaning in these symbolic images disconnected from reality.

A television interview sets up a verbal interaction as a performance, not only because of the semiology of the image (the positioning of the participants and the camera shots are aimed at conveying 'meaning') but because of the way the actors interpret the situation: interviewers and interviewees are influenced first by the 'camera' phenomenon and the recording of the sound and the picture (the public, reproducible aspect of the interaction), which makes their performance more formal, but also by live broadcasting, which does not allow botches and second tries. They are careful about their role and about maintaining their image by controlling the speech and body attitudes.

CONCLUSION

This chapter is not intended to represent all that takes place in media and communications education in France. Rather, it illustrates a particular approach: as a case study it shows how a discipline can be utilised to analyse a particular media form and to link media texts to the context of their production, and to the way in which language is enacted by the body. It provides an example of the concerns of one important section of those teaching the subject in France.

NOTES

1 I do not claim that gestural language and proxemic positions are always totally part of unconscious processes, but I think that customarily, and for the most part, they are.
2 These are Schegloff's 'continuers': little half-voiced expressions uttered by the interlocutor, coming as background to the speaker's turn, to show that he is 'following all right', and that the speaker may continue.

REFERENCES

Brown, P. and Levinson, S. (1978) 'Universals in language usage: politeness phenomena', in E. Goody (ed.) *Questions and Politeness*, London and New York: Cambridge University Press.
Durkheim, E. (1915) *The Elementary Forms of Religious Life*, trans. Joseph Ward Swain, London: George Allen & Unwin.
Goffman, E. (1967) *Interaction Ritual*, New York: Anchor Books.
Rolot, Christian (1986) *La communication inachevée, (thèse d'état)* University of Sorbonne Nouvelle, Paris.
Rolot, Christian and Ramirez, F. (1988) *Elire un président*, Paris: Ramsay.

Part III

Chapter 14

Theory and practice in media education
Knowing why, knowing how

David French and Michael Richards

The relationship between theory and practice, education and training, employment and vocationalism, was an important issue to
emerge from the conference which spawned this book. These sets
of dichotomies suggest opposing sets of interests held by different
groups of professionals involved in media management and production and media education. They focus on a simplified dichot-
omy between what higher education provides in terms of
intellectual development, and the specific training needs of the
industries in which the some of graduates of communication and
media studies will ultimately work.

These dichotomies, suggesting a mismatch between education
and employment, between university curricula in communication
and media studies and the requirements of media industries and
employers, are a survival of former times and attitudes. There was
a perceived gap between education and the world of work, in
which the needs of media industries were not being met by the
critical orientation to media prominent in university curricula. It
was believed by many practitioners that education for critical
awareness had taken precedence over 'knowing how to do', over
practical applications. One of the consequences of this was an
apparent privileging of theory over practice, echoing the traditional social class divisions reflected in distinctions between
mental and manual labour. Thus there was a perceived gap
between the skills and abilities of communication and media studies graduates and the skills needed in people who were to be of
immediate use to the media industries.

So, the training needs of the media industries have been contrasted with the distanced academic criticism provided by university curricula, and the two have been seen to be not only

incompatible but in conflict. However, training is becoming less narrowly defined as a result of changes in the media industries themselves, where needs are now more varied and quickly changing, where understanding of processes and principles, and transferable skills have become more important. Increasingly the new rhetoric of competencies and outcomes reflects the needs which employees are required to meet as they enter the changing media industries.

There is evidence for a developing convergence between the needs of the media industries and the skills and knowledges provided by university curricula in media studies, namely that both show an increased emphasis on the application of knowledge, rather than on the training of skills, but this convergence stops short of a recognition of a common ground where mutual needs can be identified. The obstacle to this convergence is that education and the industries both wish to define what this common ground is. The search for common ground might have an initial attractiveness, but on closer examination has proved to be unattainable. For whilst the media industries would argue that it is important that graduates have experience of the processes that underpin the production of the commodities which the media are concerned with, and this might include skills in photography, filmmaking and video production, plus an understanding of the economics and legal frameworks within which media industries work, by contrast, academics would recognise these dimensions as part of the realities of day-to-day practices in media operations but would stress the importance of a non-functional, non-utilitarian critical approach to their study whose quality should be judged on the depth of critical engagement demonstrated by students and not on the range of practical skills and 'know how' acquired.

But if this is a legitimate claim, then how is it to be provided in media studies curricula? The answer is largely through project work or placement activity which, whilst having significant virtues in exposing students to a variety of learning processes, encouraging collaboration, the use of initiative, and skills in time management, remain often a fragmented part of the curriculum, insufficiently integrated into theoretical practices. Although there are variations in different European countries this is nevertheless accentuated by a marked division of labour amongst staff in communication and media studies courses whereby the practical hands-on elements are taught by a different constituency of staff from those who teach the more prestigious theoretical and conceptual parts of course. In short, there is a class-based division of labour in the communications and media studies curriculum which reflects the tension between theory and practice.

The control of the curriculum and this division of labour remain in the hands of the university. This is so because quality assurance processes relating to course development and course review are controlled by the academy. Panel membership for course review and validation events, whilst occasionally containing practitioners, is nevertheless determined by the academy. In addition external examiners for courses, some of whom may be practitioners, are nevertheless nominated and approved by academics.

However, current circumstances offer an opportunity for the emergence of fruitful relationships between such education and the changing media industries. Nevertheless, the fact that these circumstances may be in some ways favourable to the development of education/industry links does not imply that all is straightforward, for the history of relationships between education and industry, the entrenched attitudes towards training which are prevalent in the traditional media industries and the assumptions which dominate government thinking about education and vocationalism all provide important obstacles. Above all, the hostility that has sometimes characterised the relationship between professional practice and critical media research provides important lessons for the future.

The history of undergraduate education in communication and media studies has in many ways followed in the slipstream of communication research. Until fairly recently, this general proposition has remained true of the relationship with the media industries. The tense relationship with industry, which characterised the growth of research activity in the field, spilled over into the formative years of British undergraduate education in communication and media studies and is found elsewhere in Europe. The situation in Britain can be used to illustrate the broad principles of this relationship.

Concerns with the application of research have opened a dialogue with practitioners and media organisations. But undergraduate education in communication and media studies has developed a dynamic of its own, in which an interactive dialogue with industry is being constructed. Although the two aspects of academic work are moving in the same direction, it is important that the differences between them are recognised.

Communications research has displayed continual tension and mutual reservation between academics and industrial practitioners. To quote a well-known comment by Paul Lazarsfeld, a founding figure in audience research:

> If there is any one institutional disease to which the media of mass communications seem particularly subject, it is a nervous reaction to criticism. As a student of mass media I have been continually struck and occasionally puzzled by this reaction, for it is the media themselves which so vigorously defend principles guaranteeing the right to criticize.
>
> (Lazarsfeld 1948: 123)

Such sensitivity on the part of the industry is loosely paralleled by the continuing use in academic circles of the administrative/ critical distinction as a basis for classifying research. This distinction attempts to classify research into that which is wholly subordinate to the immediate requirements of industry and that which stands back, dealing with basic issues often calling into question both the routine assumptions of practitioners and the institutional structures in which they work. It has obscured the emergence of policy as a major orientation in communication and media studies, an orientation which shares with 'administrative' research its concern to contribute to real decision-making, but which also displays some of the key features of 'critical' research, most obviously its willingness to engage in debates about fundamental goals and values.

Lazarsfeld's diagnosis of nervousness as a chronic industrial ailment can be easily documented. In part it reflects the normal reluctance of any group to see their taken-for-granted assumptions exposed to outside scrutiny, exacerbated by the exposed public position occupied by the main media organisations.

Goldie's review of Phillip Elliott's study *The Making of a Television Series* (1972) is a case in point. While not overtly hostile to research scrutiny, Goldie expressed strong views about the qualifications required by the successful researcher, stressing

> the need for the training of any research worker who hopes to study mass communication to include a period of practical work within a broadcasting organisation. Only the practical

experience of trying to do the job will give him a real insight into the purposes and practices of making television programmes.

(Goldie 1972: 517)

At the risk of over-simplifying the argument, one reading of this might suggest that research scrutiny is acceptable only if researchers become 'insiders'. As Croll and Golding (1972) usefully pointed out, this view is in striking contrast with the assumption that, in a time far shorter than the minimum for a conventional academic research, journalists expect to be able to interpret the most sensitive and complex of events. Such a conflict between expectations of researchers and journalists, both professional outsiders to the groups which they report upon, is testimony to Lazarsfeld's accuracy.

Responses to the work of the Glasgow University Media Group (1981) show the heat which can be generated in conflicts between researchers and practitioners. In replying to a study largely focusing on the Labour leadership election of 1980, Peter Sissons and Paul McKee on behalf of Independent Television News (broadcast on Channel 3) wrote:

ITN submits that the findings of the Glasgow University Media Group came close to being a political tract, with material being selected quite unscrupulously to substantiate its main beliefs. For this to masquerade as academic work is the greatest disservice that can be done to any conscientious researcher. We invite any open and fairminded observer to judge us on *all* the facts, not a selection of them.

(Sissons and McKee 1981: 12; authors' emphasis)

In claiming that 'the major stories . . . were inaccurate constructions' and that 'political news was not much more than a sectarian attack on the Left', the Glasgow University Media Group hardly conceal the political dimensions of this analysis or their conflict with the professional self-image of the news teams. These examples testify to the ferocity of this exchange and to the perpetuation of Lazarsfeld's 'institutional disease'. But it should be noted that Sissons and McKee do not object to research per se, and, indeed, they attempt to rebut the Glasgow allegations through research evidence of their own. Perhaps, by the early 1980s, and after a lengthy illness, Lazarsfeld's patient was showing signs of recovery.

Until recently, Lazarsfeld's 'administrative/critical' distinction has been accepted as a basis for classifying research. The survival value of this schema is bizarre, given its inherent definitional crudity. It seeks to draw a distinction in terms of the attitudes of researchers to the institutions they study. Administrative research, according to Lazarsfeld (1941: 2–3), assumes 'that modern media of communication are tools handled . . . for given purposes' and that 'it is the task of research to make the tool better known and thus to facilitate its use.' The goals of the media organisation or of media users are accepted as given and the purpose of the research is to facilitate their achievement.

All authorities seem to agree that critical research is far more difficult to define. In its earliest usage, for example in the work of Adorno and Horkheimer (1972) and others associated with the Frankfurt School, it represented a radical disenchantment with the mass media and their role in modern society, and to have looked for practical outcomes, in terms of contributions to debate about developments within contemporary media institutions, would have jarred with many of its fundamental commitments. But even then the position was not entirely consistent, as is reflected in Adorno's brief period in Lazarsfeld's Princeton Radio Research Project, with its dependency on commercial sponsorship and its willing acceptance of 'administrative' projects. The difficulty of achieving an unambiguous definition of critical research remains, and for Halloran (1981: 168) 'it could be argued that the main unity of the critical approach . . . is in its opposition to conventional work rather than in any more shared positive approach.'

The debate about critical and administrative research has been a continuing controversy in communication and media studies. It reflects a genuine fear of the corrupting effects of too close a dependence upon industrial sponsors. Such dependence is conceived as, for example, seducing the researcher away from theory towards rampant empiricism, away from a proper recognition of the relationship between communication processes and society, towards a naive acceptance of 'communication problems' as defined by those with an interest in particular solutions. From a rival viewpoint, critical research is sometimes conceived of as achieving its theoretical purity only at the cost of isolation from real world problems in an ivory tower of academic abstractions.

We would suggest, following Kurt Lang (1979), amongst other authorities, that the binary opposition between critical and administrative research misrepresents the current state of work in communication and media studies and, arguably, over-simplifies its past.

The difficulty in defining 'critical research', as confronted by Halloran and others, reflects the breadth of the research agenda which is left after the exclusion of work which can justifiably be defined as 'administrative'. In turn, this reflects the fact that the goals of media organisations, which 'administrative research' is supposed to accept as given, are rarely matters of agreement within the mainstream media organisations or between the various outside groups which may constitute the users of the media.

In other words, the collection of purely quantitative data about television audiences may be accurately construed as 'administrative research'. But it is difficult to find much else which does not have in some way initially to confront the ambiguities within the conflict between the various goals which are held out to media institutions, and argued over by their personnel.

A good example of this could be found in the Independent Broadcasting Authority's studies of audience attitudes to broadcasting (IBA 1987). Viewer attitudes to television are complex, seemingly inconsistent. They mirror the real tensions within the 'inform, educate and entertain' credo of the broadcasters. Researchers cannot shirk from grappling with such conflicts and inconsistencies. This questioning of the goals of broadcasting makes such work, by definition, 'critical', a classification which is bizarre indeed, given that not only is it paid for by a broadcasting organisation but it is carried out by its own staff members. The growth of policy as a research theme has led to new controversies. Often these are precisely about the dangers of subordinating research to institutional vested interests.

Garnham and Blumler engaged in just such a polemical debate over the latter's *Challenge of Election Broadcasting* (1978). But even in the heat of controversy, Garnham notes a core of agreement:

> I support Blumler's desire to relate research to the actual hurly-burly of policy, against those who would see their science as a value-free positivistic activity which merely accurately describes a world progressing independently beyond the confines of their ivory towers.
>
> (Garnham 1979: 24)

Similarly, both would agree with Gerbner's stricture that researchers in communications policy should not be 'just hired hands but men and women prepared and free to scrutinize the ends as well as the means of any project' (Gerbner 1983). Put differently, the problem for policy research is that it has to maintain sufficient independence for its findings to be taken seriously, but, on the other hand, its mission is to make proposals which are capable of stimulating change in the practices and institutions which it studies. Potentially this draws it into a very close relationship with, even a dependency upon, these institutions.

The way out of the dilemma, for the best policy research, has been to demonstrate the practical utility of considering fundamental questions. To quote the old saying, 'there is nothing so practical as a good theory'. In times like the present, when the media worldwide are undergoing fundamental change and reassessment, the audience for such views is uniquely receptive. The growth of policy research approximately coincides with the development of British communication and media studies education and it is notable that there are resemblances in the way each has confronted the issue of relationship to industry.

Communication and media research in the early 1980s was, therefore, at a crossroads. It had begun to emphasise the applications of knowledge but was handicapped by a history often represented as a division between craven subservience and open hostility to industry. But this was the time in which communication and media studies as a teaching activity was coming to maturity in Britain. The earliest courses had produced several cohorts of graduates and a second generation was becoming established. Initially, these courses had followed the assumptions then dominant in research. But the dynamics of undergraduate provision have ensured that progress away from that limiting position has been made rather more quickly than might have been expected.

Teaching in communication and media studies is about the production of graduates who must know about the field in which they have been educated, even if they will not be equally familiar with all its parts. If undergraduates are not to be the academic equivalent of schizophrenic quick-change artistes, the various traditions and specialisms have to be located on a single overall map. If the old administrative/critical distinction has any value at all, then both positions have to be considered in education as must the continuities and conflicts between them and the emergence of the newer areas of policy debate.

But there are more concrete issues than these. Where do communication and media studies graduates go after college and, even more saliently, where do they hope to go? A major career target is the media industries, broadly conceived, and students are naturally impatient that their studies should be relevant to this ambition.

This is not to suggest that all students are identically motivated or that they do not appreciate the role of theoretical, critical, components in their courses. But where pay-off in terms of an address to concrete real-world problems is available, students expect that it should be achieved. This is not unreasonable, any more than is the expectation that a communication or media studies course should have as one of its main objectives – although not the only one – the equipping of students with knowledge relevant to their subsequent ambitions.

For both of these reasons, the need to make coherent sense of the whole field and the career ambitions of students, undergraduate education has to give even more attention than does research to the practical applications of critical analysis.

But communication and media studies courses must not be drawn into a position as the teaching equivalent of administrative research, concentrating purely on the development of problem-solving communication skills. Any movement in this direction would be counter-productive, misrepresenting the fluid nature of a field in which a crucial question which has to be asked of any 'communication problem' is: 'for whom is it a problem?' Furthermore, no longer can we expect, if we ever could, single 'establishment' answers to such questions. Equally importantly, to move in the direction of communication problem-solving would sell short the potential for 'a challenge to unthinking acceptance' and 'the possibility of conscious control and deliberate change' which Gerbner (1983) saw as the key contribution of critical communication and media studies. The unique selling point of the communication and media studies graduate is an ability to locate immediate problems in a theoretically informed understanding of communication processes.

However, such arguments are incomplete unless linked to an analysis of the particular historical forms which have arisen in the relationship between British higher education and industry and of recent government attitudes to this relationship.

Government has been, and remains, committed to enhancing the vocational orientation of British higher education. Vocationalism implies that the courses students follow should in some senses equip them for careers and the world of work. It is an argument about relevance. But there are different views as to what counts as relevant preparation. Here we can distinguish between narrow 'skills training', and vocationally relevant education. Narrow training aims to reproduce quite specific, often technical, skills and techniques for a given occupation clearly located in a specific industry. On the other hand, education in communication studies has often been seen as removed from the production of directly usable skills and techniques, with its academic emphasis, critiques of practice, interests in relationships between media and the state and with policy, and so on. Within this panorama the appeal of training is clear.

Training should allow employers to match manpower with current organisational goals and practices. The skills which the trained bring are supposedly identifiable, so it is clear to employers what these employees are trained to deliver and how they can profitably be used. Education, on the other hand, has traditionally been perceived as less specific in the competencies it delivers. But a highly specific training orientation with an emphasis on current practice, skills and expertise creates serious problems for communication and media studies, its graduates and their employers.

The immediate reason for this is that the employment structure of the communications industries, their institutions and their working practices are changing at an unprecedented rate. The following are some of the key characteristics of the process and its relationship to education:

- Skills training is based on an assumption that the institutional environment will remain broadly stable. It is, after all, this environment which defines the relevance of particular skills and the appropriate levels of proficiency. At times of institutional change, more open forms of education will have a more prominent role.
- With technological change many of the traditional media skills have gone. The increasingly user-friendly new technologies require less training time and will permit the employment of recruits with the skills of the generalist able to develop in response to a wide range of specific needs.

- The pace of technological change, allied with international moves towards increased privatisation, has brought media policy into a more prominent position in public political debate. More than technical skills are needed if this situation is to be comprehended and maximum advantage gained from the opportunities it offers.

- The wide-spread use of communication technologies and the increasing recognition of the importance of optimising communication strategies has given media use a prominent role in what would conventionally have been regarded as non-media organisations. Arguably, indeed, the boundary between media and non-media organisations has been eroded. As a result, the role of traditional training schemes, with their orientation towards print journalism and mainstream television, has diminished.

- Similarly, as the economic basis of those dominant media organisations which have been the venue for traditional communication training is eroded, then other institutions may step into the gap. If a more open form of education is indeed becoming more relevant, then colleges currently providing communication and media studies courses are well placed to take up the opportunity.

- As the communications and media industries attempt to sell a wider range of often new products to new markets, their need for staff with a broad understanding of communication processes will become more acute. For example the differential success of Prestel and video-cassette recorders can only be understood in terms of a knowledge of the audience, its attitudes, use of leisure time, economic resources, and so on.

- Changes affecting the traditional media structures have radically changed the job market for graduates. For example, in broadcasting there will be a much larger number of employers as the number of production companies increases and young people are less likely than in the past to go into one institutional form of broadcasting as employees for their entire careers.

The problem for educators is to achieve the right balance in communication and media studies courses between general educational aims, the development of particular skills and vocational relevance. The promotion of critical practice in courses remains

important because of its capacity to provide an informed awareness of the needs of industry, particularly in orienting students to
problem recognition and problem-solving.

The development of critical analysis is an essential component
of vocational education and is recognised as such by many professional bodies. Nevertheless, some employers feel that students
can leave courses with a poorly conceived and developed range
of skills that do not appear to be of value, immediately or in the
long term. These perceived absences and narrow definitions of
vocationalism are problems for higher education generally and
are not unique to communication and media studies.

Many of these tensions between theory and practice have been
alluded to in the national chapters earlier in this book. Saeys
points out that in Flanders the subject Press and Communication
Science has been interpreted as a preparation for a journalistic
career, and that the institutes of applied communication which
grew up in Flanders in the 1970s were established to meet an
existing need for practical, practice-oriented education, relevant
to the job market. She argues that these new institutions and their
curricula were a response to complaints about lack of practical
knowledge that university graduates in communication science
possessed. But the solution is not an easy one. As Saeys points
out: 'It is true, however, that even though a theoretical education
devotes a lot of time to "why" questions, one needs to remain
fully aware that the majority of graduates find a job in the "how"
practice.' Practice does not figure largely in university curricula in
applied communications and media studies in Flanders. She
argues, indeed, that the universities offer

> a rather limited number of applied communication courses
> taught by professional practitioners. The confrontation with
> practical situations in controlled circumstances is considered to
> yield interesting elements within a university curriculum, but
> this may not be allowed to detract from the theoretical orien-
> tation, the fundamentally scientific and critical view trained on
> the media situation.

The tension between theory and practice is sometimes seen to be
resolvable through 'striking a balance'. Referring to the Communication Science curriculum at the University of Ghent, Saeys points
out that: 'During the development of this new curriculum, the aim
was to strike a balance between the theoretical and practical

subjects.' This suggests that the solution to the tension is the satisfying of honour, a compromise, an equality of contribution.

Heuvelman expresses the theory/practice divide as an issue in Holland centring on the need for communication managers, that is, people who combine knowledge and skills in communication theories with knowledge and skills in management theories. He argues that students in Holland are not trained to become professional communicators in the sense that professional skills in journalism, graphic design, film-making and so on are taught at schools of higher vocational education and academies of art and not in universities. Whilst there is a need for skilled trained personnel, Heuvelman argues that the increasing competition in Dutch television demands a more market-oriented approach to broadcasting which will require highly qualified people as managers. These people, he suggests, must be qualified in terms of communication theories and strategies, should be research-oriented, and should have a knowledge of the economics of broadcasting and of laws and regulations, as well as possessing management abilities. According to Heuvelman, several problems have arisen between management and programme-makers in that the former are concerned with audience ratings and audience size, but have no ideas about programme development, and know nothing of programme-making, yet decide on programme development policy.

A similar point is made by Alvarez when she suggests that:

> The communications phenomenon involves constantly changing and dynamic demands which require professionals who are able to consider communications as a strategic resource in companies or institutions; who can carry out analytic work in the production procedures in the sectors of communications, information and their reception; who are able to design communications policies and show the users how best to utilise the means of communication.

Winkin's chapter reveals an intriguing tension played out within a particular department of communication between academic and professional goals. It reveals the reluctance – perhaps in an extreme form – of academia to acknowledge the role of practitioners as equals in course provision, and more particularly illustrates an attempt to define away their relevance by imposing a narrow set of academic criteria on which to judge the value of any contribution to the quality of courses. In this way, media professionals and practitioners not only have to be competent in those professional roles, they also have to match the academic qualifications of their university-based colleagues teaching theoretical courses. Winkin's chapter demonstrates how the apparent espousal of vocational and professional goals in an academic department can be used to shore up its future politically, although the realities of such programmes can be that academics writing them have 'a vague, naive and amateurish idea of the realities of the media'. Practitioners are invited to proffer the inner secrets of their art, but are not incorporated into the day-to-day life of the department, nor into decision-making processes. As Winkin suggests 'the university is still a fortress, power lies within'.

So, practice can be introduced into theoretically oriented courses, but often as a low-status activity which remains so if students are prepared to acquiesce to this stratification between theoretical knowledges and practical skills, and to offer no resistance or place no collective pressure on the teaching department to amend its curricula. The events described in Winkin's chapter are, of course, not replicated everywhere else. Nevertheless, they illustrate some of the key factors that can influence the relationship between theory and practice within a course. The case of Liège demonstrates how it is possible to utilise broadly accepted vocational and professional goals to shore up an educational philosophy which is quite at odds with those goals, if at the same time those doing so have the power to determine the educational agenda from within, a power which allows them to resist pressures from professionals from outside and to deflect and possibly demobilise students from within.

The relationship between theory and practice, between academics and media practitioners, remains one of the major driving forces in communications and media education. It is fuelled as a potentially major influence by changes in media industries themselves, the development of global media and by changes in higher education systems. It is an area of productive tension, to some degree a site of struggle for control and influence. Academia will continue to resist control of curricula from outside and attempts to allow short-term employment needs to shape those curricula. At the same time, the communication and media industries will not remain silent and will continue to raise questions about the relevance of communication and media education to their needs.

REFERENCES

Adorno, T. and Horkheimer, M. (1972) *The Dialectic of Enlightenment*, New York: Herder & Herder, pp. 120–67.

Blumler, J. G., Gurevitch, M. and Ives, J. (1978) *The Challenge of Election Broadcasting*, Leeds: Leeds University Press.

Croll, P. and Golding, P. (1972) 'The sociology of television', *The Listener*, 26 October: 541.

Elliott, P. (1972) *The Making of a Television Series*, London: Constable.

Garnham, N. (1979) 'Politics and the mass media in Britain: the strange case of Dr Blumler', *Media, Culture and Society* 1(1), January: 23–4.

Gerbner, G. (1983) 'The importance of being critical – in one's own fashion', *Journal of Communication*, 33(3), Summer: 355–62.

Glasgow University Media Group (1981) 'The bias in the television image', *New Statesman*, 23 January: 6–8.

Goldie, G. W. (1972) 'The sociology of television', *The Listener*, 19 October: 517–19.

Halloran, J. (1981) 'The context of mass communication research', in D. Whitney, E. Wartella and S. Windahl (eds) (1982) *Mass Communication Review Yearbook*, Vol. III, Beverly Hills, London and New Delhi: Sage, pp. 163–205.

IBA (1987) *Attitudes to Broadcasting in 1986*, London: IBA.

Lang, K. (1979) 'The critical functions of empirical communication research', *Media, Culture and Society*, 1 January: 83–96.

Lazarsfeld, P. (1941) 'Remarks on administrative and critical communications research', *Studies in Philosophy and Social Science*, 9: 2–16.

—— (1948) 'The role of criticism in the management of mass media', in T. Burns (1977) *The BBC: Public Institution and Private World*, London and Basingstoke: Macmillan, p. xv.

Sissons, P. and McKee, P. (1981) 'Legal, decent and honest', *New Statesman*, 20 March: 12.

Chapter 15

Communication and media education
A new discipline in Europe?

David French and Michael Richards

The national chapters in this volume demonstrate two features which make the study of communication distinctive as an academic subject.

First is its extremely rapid growth. From a position in the 1970s with a small number of students at a very few universities, the situation is now one in which the subject is a normal part of the undergraduate provision in most European countries. Not all institutions offer it but very many do and the demand from potential students is intense and still growing. An important part of this change is that more and more the field is being taught as a single subject rather than as a subordinate part of other degree programmes.

A parallel process, of the growth of the subject and its acquisition of a distinct academic identity, has taken place in research. Direct measures of research activity are not easy to construct, but a good general indicator may be taken from publishing. While some years ago the few books produced in communication were scattered widely through the catalogues of publishers, now, in Britain at least, they are routinely given a separate section in which both classic studies and many new titles are to be found.[1]

The second, and more important, feature upon which many of the contributors to this volume agree is that the subject is peculiar in having been led in its expansion by undergraduate teaching programmes. It has grown because of the demand for courses from students. Much of the publishing activity, in which research finds expression, has had the purpose of providing teaching materials for undergraduate courses and has been economically viable because of the expansion of these courses. In the present difficult economic circumstances, with European governments often harshly pruning their research budgets and the media industries frequently preferring short-term, strictly instrumental, investigations, a vacuum has been created which has made the undergraduate market, as a source of both supply and demand, particularly important. The teachers of undergraduates produce, in their spare time, much of the research and the students, and libraries catering for them, buy many of the publications.

The purpose of this chapter is to consider the process of development of the subject and, in particular, the part which teaching programmes will be able to play in this process.

We will suggest that the contribution of teaching to the development of the field has been a positive one, and that it is likely to remain a kept motor force in its further expansion. But the role of teaching is likely to change as the field moves further along the continuum from loosely defined subject area to fully fledged discipline.

SUBJECT AREA OR DISCIPLINE?

The field of communication is developing from a subject area towards becoming a discipline. That much can be confidently and justifiably asserted. But it is essential that the complexities and ambiguities of this transition are recognised; it would certainly be wrong to see the two as either/or alternatives. There is a large middle ground between subject area and discipline and it is unclear how long, or how straightforward, is passage through it.

This chapter is not primarily an excursion into the general sociology of academic knowledge. But a few remarks about the nature of disciplines are essential if the process is to be clarified.

Disciplines, in our view, are not chiefly defined by the body of knowledge over which they acquire property rights. Of course all disciplines do assume ownership of their own intellectual territory. But to arbitrate on the boundaries between the terrains of contingent disciplines would require the skills of the science fiction writer. Territorial overlaps are common, or at least they would be if sensible maps could be drawn up.[2] Unfortunately for the intellectual cartographer, the ways in which rival disciplines define their own areas are often fundamentally different. Sociology and psychology, for example, seem half the time to be occupying the same space, but constructing it differently, like the denizens of the 'other worlds' of science fiction.

To short-cut the argument, our proposition is that disciplines are at root reflexive: they are defined by a fundamental consensus among their members. This consensus is about the terrain within which debate, controversy and inquiry takes place: conflict is, paradoxically, at its heart. However, those to whom the terrain belongs share something which makes sense to them but which is not open to objective definition in a way which is transparent to, and acceptable by, those in neighouring fields.

Furthermore, the terrain which a discipline lays claim to will change with time. In communication, the early audience studies of Lazarsfeld and his colleagues provide a case in point. Lazarsfeld, in his initial work,[3] clearly defined himself as a psychologist but it was not long before his insights were appropriated by sociologists and political scientists. Similar examples from the natural sciences abound.

In other words, to seek to define an academic discipline in terms of its most immediately obvious feature, the body of ideas and applications about which its members write, argue and teach, is inherently mistaken. It is the members themselves and the way in which they, throughout their interactions, construct this shared culture that constitute the discipline.

If we wish to understand what it is that moves academic fields from subject areas to disciplines we must look at the members and their interactions. Crucially, do they take each other, at the expense of outsiders, as their key intellectual reference groups?

Our purpose here is not to attempt to define how far the study of communication and the media has advanced towards the status of a discipline. National experiences, as will be clear from this book, vary considerably. But although the reflections of our limited group of participants offer a pointer, to achieve a credible conclusion would require a major international investigation. This is not the type of project most likely to attract funding now or at any other foreseeable time. But we do seek to promote the view that this is the direction in which the field is moving and that the future of communication and media teaching should be seen in this light.

One limiting factor in the process is the extreme difficulty which those working in the nascent discipline have in agreeing upon its name. Given that semiotics has been a key force in its foundation, and that a fundamental semiotic proposition concerns the import-ance of names, this is not an unimportant problem. Among the titles currently in use in European universities are: 'Communication Science', 'Communication Studies', 'Information Science', 'Media Studies', 'Cultural Studies' and 'Information and Communication'.

It is evident that some of these variations represent difficulties of translation. The two key words 'information' and 'communication' mean quite different things even in English and French, let alone in other European languages. Similarly the distinction between 'communication' and 'media' changes as linguistic frontiers are crossed. A term like 'communication science,' widely acceptable in other European countries, runs into difficulties in Britain where the overt use of 'science' for the study of social and cultural processes has become fraught with confusion to the point of controversy.

But the difficulties are more than ones of translation. Indeed the fact that an act of translation is necessary is revealing. Physics, sociology, chemistry, psychology, all emerged as new names alongside their disciplines and hardly change in different languages. We do not have that advantage. If there is to be an internationally shared name, our field has yet to discover it. For now it has to live with a variety of names that reflect the particular nuances of the different national and institutional contexts in which it has grown.

If the workers in the field do not share a name, they do, however, share certain common founding questions. Across Europe most relevant departments and research units were set up to teach and study questions concerning the relation between the mass media and society: the way in which media texts are produced, their nature and form, and their reception by audiences. In different situations only the emphasis would vary between a concern with media effects, with media literacy or with the preparation of informed as well as skilled recruits for the communication industries.[4]

But, as already noted, emerging disciplines progressively take control of their subjects, moulding them to suit their own agenda. Precisely this has happened in our field, broadening its application well beyond the founding questions which were its launch pad. There is an obvious parallel with sociology, which was able to achieve its wide-spread representation in higher education partly because of its perceived ability to address problems of 'social pathology'. Subsequently, sociology has redefined its field, successfully demonstrating its relevance well beyond the boundaries of publicly recognised social problems and, of course, also showing that such problems can only be explained in the context of a wider analysis of the society within which they are located. Work on subjects such as vandalism, drug use and football hooliganism continues to take place in sociology departments. But the approaches chosen are increasingly derived from, and evaluated by, other members of the discipline.

Similarly, in the study of communication, the founding questions reflected broad social anxieties about the perceived effects of the media in general or of particular media texts. Initially such questions were addressed in terms of simple causal models in which the variables were straightforwardly derived from 'obvious' social processes. But now, when such questions arise as research topics, the models are far more sophisticated and the answers produced are more subtle; questions are phrased more in terms of how audience members use the media in complex social processes in which they are only one among a plurality of cultural sources. The old, common-sensical, 'hypodermic' model of cause and effect has fallen into deep academic disrepute, however popular it may remain among the public and politicians.[5]

Just as the questions which characterised the early stages of the study of communication were broadly international, so the process of redefining those questions has also transcended national frontiers. Indeed, in the search for intellectual support researchers have been forced to look abroad. A striking example from Britain is the explosion into the field of 'continental' structuralism and semiology in the 1970s and early 1980s, as a means of transcending the extreme limitations of traditional empiricist content analysis in the analysis of texts.

The argument so far is that the study of communication shows at least some of the qualities of an emerging discipline as researchers have progressively gained the strength to exert some control over the research agenda. But the process of constructing the subject is wider than this and in it the role of undergraduate teaching has been particularly important.

As has been noted, most courses in the subject began by addressing either the general question of media literacy or the perceived need to provide a particular kind of pre-professional training. In either case the focus was pre-eminently upon the major media of public communication: the press and broadcasting. For some courses, particularly those with a heavy practical emphasis, this remains the case. But very often course design has broadened. Subject such as public relations, advertising, marketing, corporate communication, communication management, even leisure, recreation and tourism, commonly occur within communication programmes.

The reasons for this are complex but the process is clear: basic insights developed in the analysis of the media are being increasingly applied to a broader range of communication and cultural processes.[6] Similarly the teaching staff responsible for such innovation are more frequently drawn from within the subject, rather than being recruited as experts purely in their field of application.

This is a process of genuinely disciplinary growth: it is quite different from the accumulation of vaguely related topics which might be found, for example, in a loose modular degree programme, organised on 'self-service' principles. In European communication a core of theory and analysis is being extended to new contexts and developed in these new contexts in ways which potentially feed back in to the original core areas. The distinctive feature is that the stimulus for such disciplinary growth is the dynamic of the teaching programme.

It is possible to speculate about some of the reasons. On the whole, teachers probably prefer to be associated with teaching programmes in a single subject rather than sharing joint honours programmes with other specialisms. There is an incentive therefore to extend and develop the subject to single honours status. Similarly, opportunities for professional preferment are associated with teaching programmes which are growing, again an incentive towards breadth of application.[7] It is also probably not unimportant that the subjects to which communication and media studies have been extended are ones which have mostly been relatively prosperous over the past decade, capable of employing many of the graduates who initially flocked to the subject in the hope of entry to the high profile, but low recruiting, professions allied to the press and broadcasting.

If this is a process of movement towards disciplinary status, in that the field is ceasing to be defined by its subject of application, but instead is becoming characterised by a core body of ideas whose application is potentially open-ended, then the following is also important. The transition is being produced, not by external forces, but by those within the field exerting control over it, taking advantage of opportunities as they arise. In other words, it is as if there were a disciplinary academy, an invisible college, with the power to determine the subject's development.[8] The distinctive quality of communication and media studies is that this academy, insofar as it exists, is largely constituted by teachers within the subject area. But the invisible colleges of academic disciplines are normally defined by a set of institutions which are only partly developed in European communication and which are in any case not particularly accessible to those who are primarily teachers.

As yet the number of European journals remains relatively low and few achieve circulation internationally. Access for authors to those American journals which are widely available in Europe can be somewhat problematic, given the differences of orientation across the Atlantic. The case with conferences is similar: those which are overtly European tend often to be rather small; major European events are infrequent. Again, the pan-European academic associations are universally highly specialised, not corresponding to the breadths of the emerging discipline.

Such institutional academic media are therefore limited; but what are the grounds for claiming that they are also relatively inaccessible to teachers?

First, there is a need to define the concept of 'teacher'. It is not as simple as might seem: many who are primarily researchers do a little – or a lot – of teaching during the normal academic year. Similarly, those whose main activity is teaching will also normally have a commitment to research, even if it has to be done in the evening and at weekends. But, although a cliché, it remains true that it is the research activity that is crucial. The badge of entry to tenured teaching posts is generally the PhD or an equivalent research record.[9] Professional advancement generally recognises eminence in research and related publications, rather than teaching proficiency.

To note the priority given to research at the expense of teaching is not new or particular to the study of communication. If it has effects which are detrimental to the education of university students, they respect neither country nor discipline. But if it is right to propose that the emerging discipline of communication has been crucially, and beneficially, affected by the contribution of teachers and teaching, then it is worth giving further thought to the status of teaching.

By teachers we mean those whose time is chiefly given over to teaching, preparation of lectures, assessment and relevant aspects of administration. A key part of the teaching function is course design and curriculum development. 'Teaching' means these tasks, whether carried out by those who are primarily teachers or by those whose principal responsibility is research. The functions have deliberately been defined in this way rather than in terms of self-conceptions: whether the individual thinks of him or herself firstly as researcher or teacher. If an implicit purpose of this chapter is to change consciousness in order more fully to recognise the strength and importance of teaching, and to ensure that this is fully drawn upon in the future of the discipline, it is essential that we are not trapped within the limitations of our own false consciousness. Many who may have learned that it is more profit- able to define themselves in terms of their research are, in our terms, to be regarded as teachers.

In most well-established disciplines it is probable that the bal- ance of intellectual effort is heavily tilted towards research rather than teaching. The latter is heavily based upon the use of textbooks as examples of the transmission of established knowledge; creativity and innovation naturally turn towards research to find their expression. But is the same true in a field which is developing as fast as communication? Probably not. Although there are of course the major classic studies and intellectual traditions which can be explained in conventional ways, the experience at least of those contributing to this book is that, in the normal work of teaching, knowledge is continually being developed and new applications sought. There is an immense force of intellectual creativity taking place across the communication teaching pro- grammes of European universities which at present finds its expression only in the relatively closed circuits of the lecture theatre and seminar room. Students when they graduate carry the message to the outside world. But is this the only appropriate dissemination mechanism?

It ought to be possible to find ways in which the creativity which goes into teaching programmes can first be recognised, by publication, and thus attributed to their originators, and then be shared by other teachers and by researchers. The trick will be to achieve this in ways which reproduce those features of the research-oriented system which are essential if institutional credi- bility is to be maintained, but to be more open to inputs derived from teaching experience. This implies not that the criteria for the selection of conference papers or the refereeing of journal articles should be relaxed but that they should be refocused. Indeed, it might not be unreasonable to focus rather more attention on the interests of the potential audiences than is often the case in papers and articles, where consumer interest is often assumed to be both excited and satisfied purely by the intrinsic quality of the piece. Maybe this cannot be achieved within existing journals and conferences: if not, then there will be a strong case for new ones to be created.

If it is correct to argue that the study of communication is moving towards becoming a fully fledged discipline, then it is essential that full attention is paid to the importance of teaching in its past and future. A key indicator of the mature discipline is the profusion of conferences and journals associated with it. If communication were to follow the conventional model, then such media would be dominated by the few full-time researchers and the 'written by candle-light' spare-time projects of the full-time teachers. The intellectual creativity produced by teachers in their mainstream work would be side-lined. For such a change to be justified it would have to be accepted that there is no generalised audience for the insights such work offers or be assumed that sufficient expression for such ideas is achieved through such indirect input into conventional research projects as may happen to trickle into place.

It has been argued in Chapter 14 that teaching has had a particularly important role in breaking down the barrier between academics and practitioners: teaching has demonstrated that a concern with applications can achieve substantive practical outcomes without either subverting academic principles or abdicating the obligation to push forward the process of intellectual creativity. The maintenance of a mutually beneficial relationship with practitioners and communication industries in general is undoubtedly an essential condition for the healthy growth of the field. It would be idle to hope that intellectual excellence alone will produce sufficient funding from governments and conventional academic sources to foster the emerging discipline. It will maximise its chances of the essential financial support only if it can demonstrate relevance to perceived commercial, cultural and social needs. If this is not to become a seriously distorting factor in the future of the field, subordinating it to the changing whims of big business and other vested interests, it is vital that academics continue to take the initiative in building and maintaining the channels of communication with the relevant institutions. Only in this way can we hope to retain some control over what passes through these channels and to ensure that the flow is a two-directional one. In this respect the approach which has been developed in teaching programmes offers a model which may be useful in the future of research.

It is clear from the varied European experiences described in this book that to generalise about the interests of practitioners in things academic is dangerous: traditions vary enormously between countries. Individuals also vary similarly: some are highly aware of new ideas bearing upon their professional practice; others may perceive them as dangerous and seek to avoid all contact. But it is probably not unreasonable to suggest that practitioners are more likely to be concerned with outcomes and applications than with basic principles and that they have a necessary interest in how their graduate recruits have been trained. If such an audience is to be addressed through the conventional disciplinary mechanisms of journals and conferences then a strong representation in these media of that middle ground between research and vocational practice, which is represented by undergraduate teaching, would be beneficial.

In sum, the propositions of this chapter are that the field of communication has expanded rapidly, it will continue to do so and will increasingly become a normal component in the portfolio of courses offered by most universities. Second, the role of undergraduate education has had a particularly important function in the development of the field. The third proposition is that the study of communication seems to be moving on a trajectory from a subject area towards becoming a discipline and the character of the discipline will reflect the role of education in its history. Finally, it is in the interests of all – teachers, researchers and practitioners – that the institutional form of the emerging discipline should continue to give space to the creative force of education and of teachers.

NOTES

1 Gryspeerdt makes a similar point about Belgium in his chapter in this volume.
2 The classic exposition of this is in Kuhn (1962).

3 The preface to Berelson, Lazarsfeld and McPhee (1954) marks a transitional point.
4 Compare the differences and similarities between the Spanish and British chapters in this book.
5 The vast literature on uses and gratifications provides many examples. See, for example, Morley (1986).
6 See Windahl and Signitzer (1992) for an example of this from outside education.
7 There are interesting parallels with the origins of psychology. See Ben-David and Collins (1966).
8 For the concept of the 'invisible college', a group of scholars interacting through the communication mechanisms of scientific disciplines, see Crane (1972). See Winkin's chapter in this collection for a dramatic illustration.
9 See Winkin, in this volume, for a dramatic example.

REFERENCES

Ben-David, J. and Collins, R. (1966) 'Social factors in the origin of a new science: the case of psychology', *American Sociological Review* 31(4): 451–65.
Berelson, B., Lazarsfeld, P. and McPhee, W. (1954) *Voting*, Chicago, IL: University of Chicago Press.
Crane, D. (1972) *Invisible Colleges*, Chicago, IL: University of Chicago Press.
Kuhn, T. S. (1962) *The Structure of Scientific Revolutions*, Chicago, IL: University of Chicago Press.
Morley, D. (1986) *Family Television: Cultural Power and Domestic Leisure*, London: Comedia.
Windahl, S. and Signitzer, B. (with Olson, J. T.) (1992) *Using Communication Theory*, London: Sage.

Name index

Subject index

underemployment 39
unemployment 41, 52, 53;
  intellectual 39
UNESCO (United Nations
  Educational, Scientific and
  Cultural Organization) 147
United States 8, 11, 43n, 61, 68–9,
  86; Hollywood Studio system
  10; 'legacy of fear' 155; Payne
  Fund studies 154; texts and
  research reports 13; theoretical
  preparation for students 36
universities 23, 65–7; ability to
  control demand for places 25;
  centralisation in 21–2, 25;
  different, competition between
  66; entrance examinations 42n,
  55; growth in sociological
  subjects 32; lack of
  differentiation 28, 30; local
  autonomy allowed to 25; new,
  emergence of 90; private 28;
  provincial, outlying 36; small,

proliferation of 42n; *see also*
  academics; courses; curricula;
  degrees; disciplines; faculties;
  students; *also under individual
  city/town names*
Uppsala University 122
Utrecht, State University 131

Valencia 52; Catholic Action
  School of Journalism 49
Växjö University 122
video 60, 180; corporate 97
video-cassette recorders 189
visual arts 33
vocational training 34, 92–3;
  communication science and
  65–71
vocationalism 188, 189, 190

Wallonia 22, 64, 114
'why' questions *see* 'know-how/
  know-why'
women 93